Making It Work

12

A Handbook for **Reading**, **Writing**, **Language**, and **Media**

Dianne Fenner
Marie Clayden
Christine McAdam
Christine Straus

Making It Work 12: A Handbook for Reading, Writing, Language, and Media

Authors
Dianne Fenner, Marie Clayden,
Christine McAdam, Christine Straus

Director of Publishing
David Steele

Publisher
Mark Cressman

Project Manager
Doug Panasis, Resources.too

Developmental Editor
Susan Petersiel Berg

Copy Editor
Susan Hughes

Indexer
Noeline Bridge

Production Coordinator
Helen Locsin

ArtPlus Production Coordinator
Dana Lloyd

Cover Design
Dave Murphy/ArtPlus Ltd.

Text Design
Alicia Countryman,
Dave Murphy/ArtPlus Ltd.

Page Layout
ArtPlus Ltd.

Technical Art
ArtPlus Ltd.

Photo Research and Permissions
Lisa Brant

Printer
Transcontinental Printing Inc.

The authors and publisher gratefully acknowledge the contributions of the following educators:

Ken Draayer, Niagara District School Board, ON

Myra Junyk, Toronto Catholic District School Board, ON

Diana Knight, Halton District School Board, ON

Catherine Logan, Toronto District School Board, ON

Mary Lou Smitheram, Upper Canada District School Board, ON

Catherine Stasiw, Toronto Catholic District School Board, ON

COPYRIGHT © 2003 by Nelson, a division of Thomson Canada Limited.

Printed and bound in Canada
1 2 3 4 05 04 03 02

For more information contact Nelson, 1120 Birchmount Road, Toronto, Ontario, M1K 5G4. Or you can visit our Internet site at http://www.nelson.com

ALL RIGHTS RESERVED. No part of this work covered by the copyright herein may be reproduced, transcribed, or used in any form or by any means—graphic, electronic, or mechanical, including photocopying, recording, taping, Web distribution, or information storage and retrieval systems—without the written permission of the publisher.

For permission to use material from this text or product, contact us by
Tel 1-800-730-2214
Fax 1-800-730-2215
www.thomsonrights.com

Every effort has been made to trace ownership of all copyrighted material and to secure permission from copyright holders. In the event of any question arising as to the use of any material, we will be pleased to make the necessary corrections in future printings.

National Library of Canada Cataloguing in Publication

Making it work 12 : a handbook for reading, writing, language and media / Dianne Fenner ... [et al.].

Includes index.

A component of Making it work 12 to be used with Moving on and Making it work 12: teacher's guide. For use in grade 12.
ISBN 0-7725-2923-X

1. Readers (Secondary) 2. English language—Composition and exercises. I. Fenner, Dianne II. Title: Moving on.

PE1408.M365 2002   428.6
C2002-905464-8

We acknowledge for their financial support of our publishing program the Canada Council, the Ontario Arts Council, and the Government of Canada through the Book Publishing Industry Development Program (BPIDP).

TABLE OF CONTENTS

How to Use this Handbook — iv

Literature Studies and Reading

The Need to Read — 2
How to Use Reading Strategies to Understand Text — 6
How to Use and Create a Table of Contents — 12
How to Use and Create an Index — 17
How to Identify Design Elements in Text — 21
How to Read Visuals in Informational Text — 25
How to Read a Business Report — 32
How to Assess and Interpret Information, Ideas, and Issues in Text — 37
How to Recognize the Perspectives of Authors and Readers — 43
How to Analyze the Role of Suspense — 49
How to Analyze the Role of Description — 54
How to Recognize Allusion and Irony — 57
How to Understand Themes in Literature — 62

Writing

Exploring Writing — 70
How to Write a Letter — 74
How to Write a Memorandum — 78
How to Create an Action Plan — 81
How to Develop and Implement a Research Plan — 85
How to Revise a Draft — 89
How to Write a Short Essay — 95
How to Cite Sources — 100
How to Prepare a Portfolio — 106
How to Write Instructions — 111
How to Write a Report for the Workplace — 115
How to Write a Poem — 120

Language

Using Your Language Competently and Confidently — 126
How to Expand Your Vocabulary — 129
How to Give Oral Instructions Effectively — 134
How to Become an Effective Listener — 138
How to Create an Effective Speaking Style — 143
How to Create and Give Effective Oral Presentations — 148
How to Communicate in a Group — 156
How to Create Your Own Voice in Writing — 162

Media Studies

Make the Connection — 168
How to Assess Information from Media — 170
How to Describe Design and Production Choices in Media — 174
How to Identify Bias in Visual, Auditory, and Print Media — 178
How to Understand and Analyze Audience Reaction — 182
How to Create a Radio Commercial — 186
How to Create a Photo Essay — 189

Grammar

Parts of speech — 194
   Nouns — 195
   Pronouns — 197
   Verbs — 200
   Adjectives — 201
   Adverbs — 203
   Conjunctions and Prepositions — 205
Sentences — 208
   Sentence Structures — 208
   Common Sentence Errors — 210
Punctuation — 212
   Ending a Sentence — 212
   Commas — 215
   Other Punctuation — 217
Connecting Words — 222
Direct and Indirect Speech — 225
Using Language — 228
   Synonyms — 228
   Antonyms — 230
   Homonyms — 231
Spelling Rules — 233

Index — 236
Acknowledgements — 240

How to Use this Handbook

Each unit of this handbook begins with an introduction to the main concepts of the unit. In each of the first four units, you will find a number of "how-to" entries that will help you attain the communications skills you need to succeed in school, in the workplace, and in the world around you. The fifth unit offers you information, support, and practice in various areas of grammar.

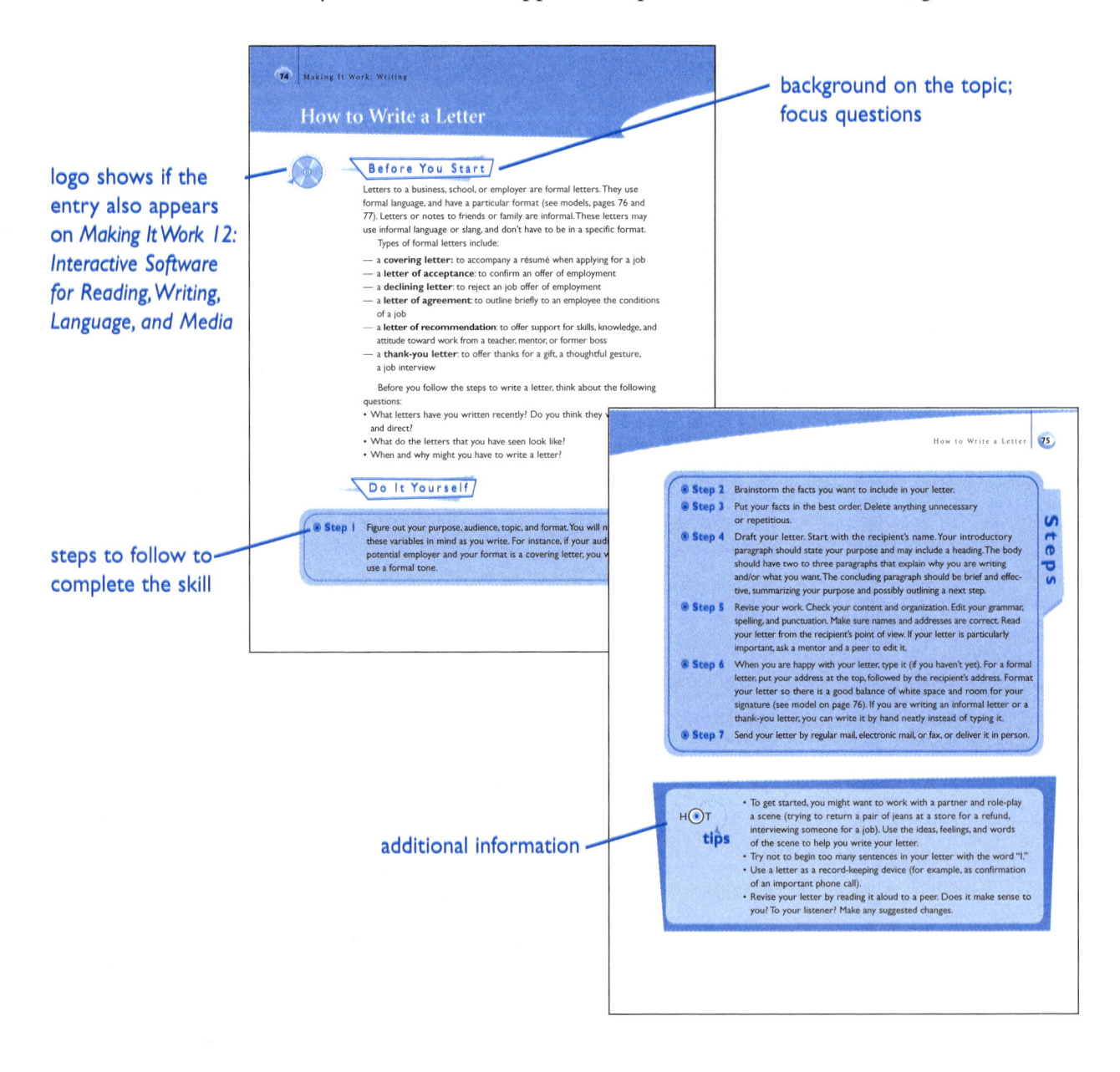

logo shows if the entry also appears on *Making It Work 12: Interactive Software for Reading, Writing, Language, and Media*

background on the topic; focus questions

steps to follow to complete the skill

additional information

Sample page: How to Write a Letter

Before You Start

Letters to a business, school, or employer are formal letters. They use formal language, and have a particular format (see models, pages 76 and 77). Letters or notes to friends or family are informal. These letters may use informal language or slang, and don't have to be in a specific format.

Types of formal letters include:
— a **covering letter**: to accompany a résumé when applying for a job
— a **letter of acceptance**: to confirm an offer of employment
— a **declining letter**: to reject an job offer of employment
— a **letter of agreement**: to outline briefly to an employee the conditions of a job
— a **letter of recommendation**: to offer support for skills, knowledge, and attitude toward work from a teacher, mentor, or former boss
— a **thank-you letter**: to offer thanks for a gift, a thoughtful gesture, a job interview

Before you follow the steps to write a letter, think about the following questions:
• What letters have you written recently? Do you think they were clear and direct?
• What do the letters that you have seen look like?
• When and why might you have to write a letter?

Do It Yourself

- **Step 1** Figure out your purpose, audience, topic, and format. You will need to keep these variables in mind as you write. For instance, if your audience is a potential employer and your format is a covering letter, you will want to use a formal tone.
- **Step 2** Brainstorm the facts you want to include in your letter.
- **Step 3** Put your facts in the best order. Delete anything unnecessary or repetitious.
- **Step 4** Draft your letter. Start with the recipient's name. Your introductory paragraph should state your purpose and may include a heading. The body should have two to three paragraphs that explain why you are writing and/or what you want. The concluding paragraph should be brief and effective, summarizing your purpose and possibly outlining a next step.
- **Step 5** Revise your work. Check your content and organization. Edit your grammar, spelling, and punctuation. Make sure names and addresses are correct. Read your letter from the recipient's point of view. If your letter is particularly important, ask a mentor and a peer to edit it.
- **Step 6** When you are happy with your letter, type it (if you haven't yet). For a formal letter, put your address at the top, followed by the recipient's address. Format your letter so there is a good balance of white space and room for your signature (see model on page 76). If you are writing an informal letter or a thank-you letter, you can write it by hand neatly instead of typing it.
- **Step 7** Send your letter by regular mail, electronic mail, or fax, or deliver it in person.

HOT tips
• To get started, you might want to work with a partner and role-play a scene (trying to return a pair of jeans at a store for a refund, interviewing someone for a job). Use the ideas, feelings, and words of the scene to help you write your letter.
• Try not to begin too many sentences in your letter with the word "I."
• Use a letter as a record-keeping device (for example, as confirmation of an important phone call).
• Revise your letter by reading it aloud to a peer. Does it make sense to you? To your listener? Make any suggested changes.

How to Use this Handbook   v

— something to think about as you read samples of the skill

— one or more samples of the result of the skill, notes identify elements of the skill

— questions about the models

— ways to apply the skill to selections in *Moving On*

— additional activities based on the skill

Page 76 — Making It Work: Writing

Here are two letters. Why is the language different in each one?

Model 1

letter set in block style, with all information beginning at the left, and each new kind of information set in its own "block" of print

addresses
Joan Albert
123 Ontario Street
Peterborough, Ontario
N2M 1X8

phone number — (705) 555-4567
e-mail address — Joanalbe@hotletter.com

date — April 29, 2002

Viola Sussex
Art Gallery Director
345 Blockline Avenue
Peterborough, Ontario
N3X 2M2

formal greeting — Dear Mrs. Sussex:
subject line — Re: Position opening at art gallery
introduction — I enjoyed meeting you at my job interview last Tuesday. Thank you very much for making the time to see me.

purpose of letter — I have not heard from you since our interview, so I thought I would send this quick note. The time I spent working at the art gallery in Curve Lake gave me a great deal of experience handling
details — many tasks during busy times, and I think I could be a real asset to your staff.

For your convenience, I am attaching another copy of my résumé. I look forward to hearing from you.

formal closing — Sincerely,
signature in blue or black pen — *Joan Albert*
Joan Albert

Page 77 — How to Write a Letter

Model 2

informal greeting — Hi Winston:
introduction — I'll never go on another blind date again. What were you thinking when you set me up with your friend Lin? We have nothing in common. She is five years older than me, lives out of town, likes classical music, and hates computers. Could anyone be more different? We had a terrible time last night. Don't ever set me up with anyone again.

details

informal closing — You were wrong on this one, but I'll still meet you tonight for the game.
Ken

Think about It

What are the two purposes of the letter on page 76? What makes each of the model letters effective?

Use the Anthology

Read "Childhood, 1916" (pages 129-133). Explain whether you think using the letters is an effective way to tell a story.

Activities

1. Write a letter to a mentor, teacher, or former employer requesting a letter of reference.
2. Write a covering letter, to accompany a résumé, for a job advertised in the newspaper. Indicate why you're the best person for the job and why you want it. Don't repeat what is in your résumé — just highlight the key points.
3. Write a thank-you letter to a relative for a birthday gift or to a friend for a thoughtful gesture.
4. Write an e-mail letter. Give only necessary information, and don't be inappropriate. Avoid overusing all-capitals (this indicates yelling). Choose an appropriate subject, and indicate the subject at the top of the letter. Use some e-mail characters, or emoticons, to get your points across: :-) for a smile/ ;-) for a wink/ :-(for disappointment.

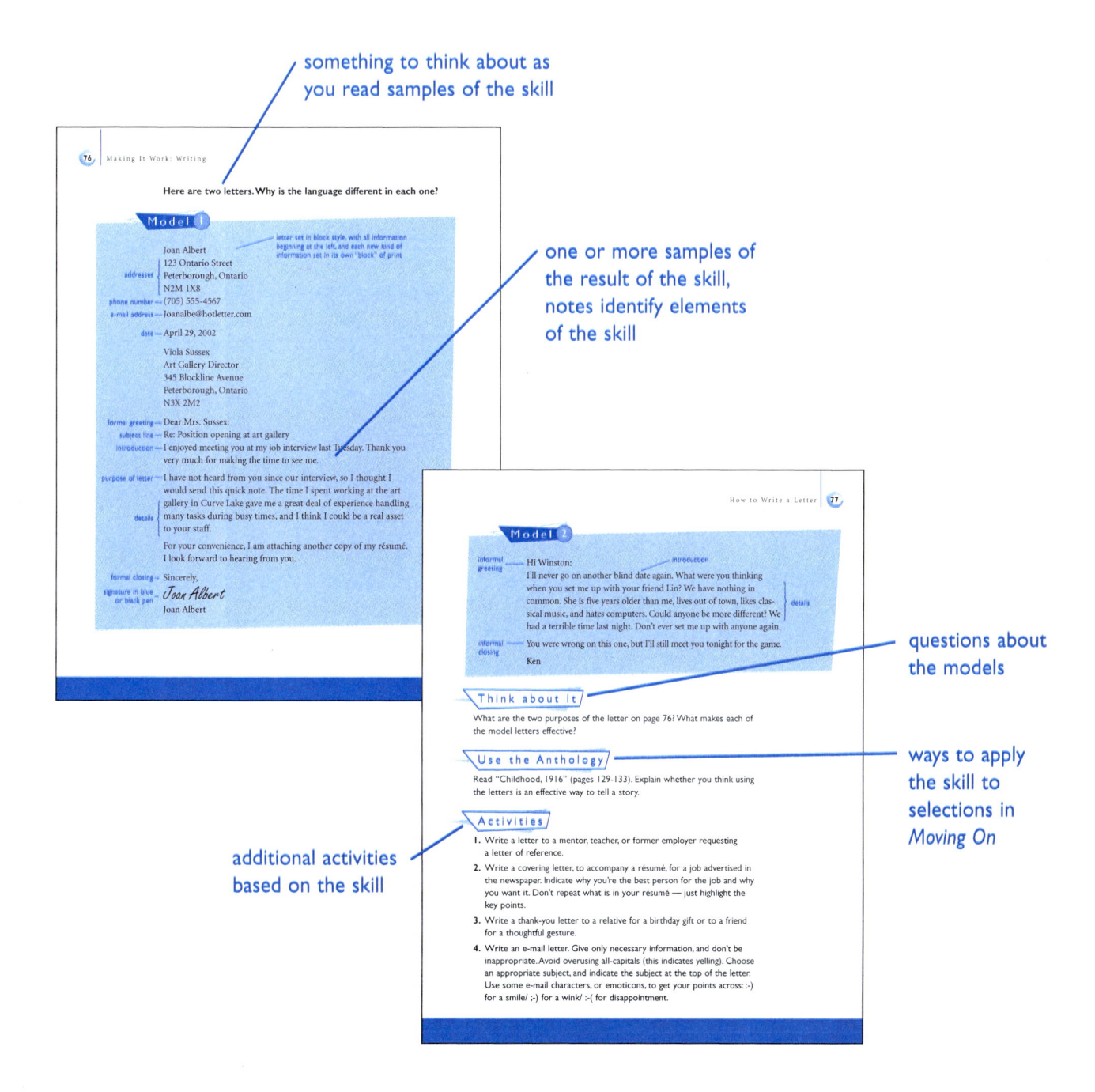

Literature Studies and Reading

TABLE OF CONTENTS

The Need to Read	2
How to Use Reading Strategies to Understand Text	6
How to Use and Create a Table of Contents	12
How to Use and Create an Index	17
How to Identify Design Elements in Text	21
How to Read Visuals in Informational Text	25
How to Read a Business Report	32
How to Assess and Interpret Information, Ideas, and Issues in Text	37
How to Recognize the Perspectives of Authors and Readers	43
How to Analyze the Role of Suspense	49
How to Analyze the Role of Description	54
How to Recognize Allusion and Irony	57
How to Understand Themes in Literature	62

The Need to Read

Recently, people who study society and social trends predicted that we soon wouldn't need to read. They thought that computers would do all of our reading and writing for us, and that we would view all text on personal data assistants (PDAs). This prediction, of course, hasn't come true. We need to read in many situations, and for many reasons. There are many purposes for reading, and a strategy to match each purpose. You will learn more about these strategies in this unit.

▸ What you read

From this checklist, consider the types of things you read in your job, your co-op placement, your school subjects, and your personal life. Get a copy of the checklist from your teacher, then circle on it the number that describes the importance of each kind of reading to you. (0 means *no importance*, 1 means *little importance*, 2 means *some importance*, 3 means *great importance*.)

Reading Form	Importance			
directions	0	1	2	3
* instructions	0	1	2	3
faxes	0	1	2	3
notes	0	1	2	3
* memos	0	1	2	3
logbooks	0	1	2	3
bulletins	0	1	2	3
* letters	0	1	2	3
manuals	0	1	2	3
* literature	0	1	2	3
* stories	0	1	2	3

*this form appears in the handbook

The Need to Read

Reading Form	Importance			
* poems	0	1	2	3
* essays	0	1	2	3
trade magazines	0	1	2	3
promotional materials	0	1	2	3
newsletters	0	1	2	3
*reports	0	1	2	3
warranties	0	1	2	3
guarantees	0	1	2	3
rules and regulations	0	1	2	3
health and safety guidelines	0	1	2	3
notices	0	1	2	3
contracts	0	1	2	3
catalogues	0	1	2	3
government regulations	0	1	2	3
pamphlets	0	1	2	3

Making It Work: Literature Studies and Reading

Reading Form		Importance		
telephone messages	0	1	2	3
supply lists	0	1	2	3
inventories	0	1	2	3
checklists	0	1	2	3
delivery information	0	1	2	3
* indexes	0	1	2	3
* tables of contents	0	1	2	3
incident reports	0	1	2	3
proposals	0	1	2	3
price quotes	0	1	2	3
activity reports	0	1	2	3
articles	0	1	2	3
flyers	0	1	2	3
marketing plans	0	1	2	3
quality reports	0	1	2	3
repair proposals	0	1	2	3
descriptions	0	1	2	3
lists of materials	0	1	2	3
phone directories	0	1	2	3
employee directories	0	1	2	3
city directories	0	1	2	3
appointment books	0	1	2	3
stock counts	0	1	2	3
labels	0	1	2	3
work schedules	0	1	2	3
atlases	0	1	2	3
floor plans	0	1	2	3

Reading Form	Importance			
forms	0	1	2	3
invoices	0	1	2	3
rate schedules	0	1	2	3
computer printouts	0	1	2	3
production sheets	0	1	2	3
work orders	0	1	2	3
signs	0	1	2	3
WHMIS posters or notices	0	1	2	3
service sheets	0	1	2	3
shift schedules	0	1	2	3
touch screens	0	1	2	3
cash registers	0	1	2	3
Web sites	0	1	2	3
e-mail messages	0	1	2	3
spreadsheets	0	1	2	3
bills	0	1	2	3
financial statements	0	1	2	3

(Taken in part from *The Ontario Skills Passport: Skills and Work Habits for the Workplace*, 2000-2001, Government of Ontario)

▸ Using what you read

Which of these forms of reading do you not recognize? Talk with a partner or do research to learn about them. Select five of the reading forms that are most important to you. Explain in a paragraph why these forms are important in your personal life or work.

Share your paragraph with other members of a group of four. Compare your selections with theirs. Which ones do you have in common? Explain why that might be so.

▸ Sampling the text

List the forms of reading that have asterisks beside them. These are the forms you will explore in depth in this handbook. Use the handbook index to find the page on which each form appears.

How to Use Reading Strategies to Understand Text

Before You Start

All readers struggle to understand text sometimes, especially when reading something new or complex. The key to understanding what you read is to have strategies to help you find meaning.

The strategies you choose will depend on the kind of text you are reading, and why you are reading it. Before you follow the steps to using different strategies to understand what you read, think about the questions below:

- What is the first thing you usually do before you read?
- What do you do while you're reading to help you understand what you are reading?
- What do you do after you read to help you understand what you have read?

Do It Yourself

Before-You-Read Strategies

Step 1 Prepare yourself to read before you start to read. Here are some strategies:

- Make a list, brainstorm ideas, or have a conversation with a partner about **what you already know** about the topic. Think about anything you have read or seen about the topic, what experiences you have with it, or what your opinions are about it.

- **Create a Know-Wonder-Learned chart** to help you understand what you read. Create one column labelled Know, one labelled Wonder, and one labelled Learned. In the first column, list what you already know about the text. In the second, list what you want to know. In the third, reflect on and list what you learned about the topic after you read.

- **Notice how the text is organized.** If you have read a similar text, think about elements that helped you find information. Look for organizing features such as a table of contents, a glossary, or an index. Think about what kind of information you can get from each of those features.

- **Prepare a Headings to Questions chart.** Make a three-column chart and add labels: Heading or Subheading, Turned into a Question, Answers Found While Reading. Record information under the appropriate headings.

- **Prepare an advance organizer.** Look at the headings and subheadings in the text. Use them to make a chart or outline of the main ideas you expect to read about. As you read, take notes about each idea in the appropriate place on the chart or outline.

- **Know your purpose and choose a reading style.** Ask yourself what your purpose is for reading the text. Is it to find specific information? You might want to scan, or look over, the text for specific words and phrases. Is it to get a general impression of the content? You might want to skim the text, or read it quickly, to get an overview of the main ideas. Is it to study or make notes? You will want to read the text closely and carefully, making notes as you go. Is it to enjoy? Read at a time and in a place where you can enjoy the text.

- Help yourself to read fluently by first looking over, or **scanning the text** for unfamiliar words and phrases. Define these words and phrases before you read (use a dictionary or ask someone who knows) so that they won't distract you from the flow of the meaning as you read.

Step 2 Have any organizers (charts, outlines, and so on) or notes with you as you begin to read.

Making It Work: Literature Studies and Reading

Do It Yourself

As-You-Read Strategies

- **Step 1** Use these strategies to make sure you understand as you read, and to help keep you focussed on meaning as you read.

  - Try to interact with the text as you read it. Ask yourself questions or make notes about what you have read at key points in the text (at the end of a section, at the end of a page, wherever a natural break in the text happens). This will help to keep the ideas alive in your mind, and will help you to connect to new ideas that you'll encounter.

  - You may find that you've lost your concentration and are losing the meaning of what you're reading. Stop reading and go back in the text to the last point or section that you understood and remember. Reread the section that has become unclear.

  - Make note of words with which you are unfamiliar, whose meaning you don't know, or which you find hard to pronounce. Find their meanings and/or pronunciations.

  - Help your comprehension by picturing what you're reading. Try creating a movie in your head to help you understand and remember.

  - If what you're reading is difficult or dense, try reducing the text to smaller, more manageable chunks. After you've read one chunk of text, reflect about it, ask questions, or make brief notes. Then go on to the next chunk and repeat the process. A Headings to Questions chart can work to help you with difficult or dense text that includes subheadings.

- **Step 2** Keep track of the facts and ideas that you learn as you read. You may wish to try these strategies:

  - Highlight important ideas and details as you read. On a photocopy or in a book that you own, highlight, underline, or circle key ideas. On a copy of a book that is not yours, use self-stick notes.

  - Make notes in the text margins, or on self-stick notes, to summarize a key point or to draw attention to it.

  - Make notes in the appropriate place on a chart or outline you have prepared in advance.

Do It Yourself

After-You-Read Strategies

- **Step 1** Read the text again if you're unsure that you've understood it. Reading it for a second time can help you feel secure that you understand the meaning.
- **Step 2** Read the notes you made while reading the text.
- **Step 3** Ask yourself whether you've achieved your purpose for reading. If you haven't, read the text again, or choose another reading strategy or text that will help you find what you need to know.
- **Step 4** Use your reading response journal to reflect about what you've read. Try to connect the ideas and information you've read with your own knowledge and experiences.
- **Step 5** Summarize the main ideas and details of what you've read in paragraph form. Use the key ideas that you've highlighted during reading to help you do this.
- **Step 6** Think critically about what you've read. Ask yourself: Is this true? Is this accurate? Is this all I need to know? Do I agree with this?
- **Step 7** Use the information and ideas from the text.

Hot tips

- Don't answer questions from memory. Look for the information in the text. If the information is not directly stated, find an appropriate section of the text and reread it. Then formulate the best answer.
- If you are reading a form or job application, read the whole form through once, including the instructions for completing it. When you have completed the form, read it again to be sure you have answered all necessary questions. Ask for help if there is something you don't understand.

This is part of a government brochure. Why do you think the bold face type was used?

Model

Being a Witness in a Criminal Trial

heading

Questions and Answers about Being a Witness

subheading

Who are the key people in a criminal trial?

In most criminal trials, you'll see the following people in the courtroom:

separate points

- The **judge** conducts the trial by making decisions on the evidence presented, interpreting the law as it applies to the case, and in general, controlling the events in the courtroom.

- The **defendant**, also called the accused, is the person on trial.

bold face type

- The **Crown attorney** is the lawyer who represents the community, and who presents evidence about the crime to the court. The Crown attorney has the responsibility of proving the accused is guilty beyond a reasonable doubt.

- The **defence counsel** is the lawyer defending the person on trial. The defence counsel tries to show that the accused is innocent, or that there is a reasonable doubt that the accused is guilty. The defence counsel also ensures that the right of the accused to a fair trial is protected.

- The **court clerk** keeps a record of the trial exhibits, administers oaths, and announces the beginning or end of court sessions.

- The **court reporter** records everything that is said at the preliminary inquiry or the trial.

- The **court security officer** handles accused persons who are in custody, helps any witness who is concerned about his or her safety, and helps maintain security in the courtroom.

Some accused persons choose to have a trial by **jury** — a group of 12 men and women called "jurors". Jurors are selected by the Crown attorney and the defence counsel. The jurors listen carefully to all the witnesses, examine the evidence, receive instructions about the law from the judge, and then decide together whether the accused is guilty or not guilty of breaking the law.

Think about It

What are some of the organizing features of the brochure? How do they help you find information?

Use the Anthology

Look at "Pros, Peers Share Youth Job-Search Secrets" (pages 118-119). Discuss with a partner which Before-You-Read strategy you would use to prepare to read it. Explain your choice.

Activity

1. Select a text that you have been assigned to read, and that you find challenging. Follow the steps below to help you read and understand the text. When you are finished reading, summarize the main ideas, or tell a partner about what you have read.

    a. Decide your purpose for reading the text, and choose an appropriate style of reading to match the purpose (for example, skim, scan, close-read).

    b. Think about what you already know about the topic, or about this type of text. If you wish, record some point form notes.

    c. Scan the text for difficult or unfamiliar words. Look up these words in the dictionary. Write each definition on a self-stick note, and place it in the text margin near the word.

    d. As you read each portion of the text, make comments to yourself about what you've read. Use self-stick notes to highlight key words, phrases, or ideas.

    e. Pay attention to parts of the text where you're losing focus. Stop, go back, and reread what you've missed.

How to Use and Create a Table of Contents

Before You Start

Finding specific information while researching can be a challenge. To find the information you need without reading an entire source, you can use organizing features of the text. One organizing feature which helps narrow a search for information is a table of contents. A table of contents is a set of pages near the beginning of the book that lists the titles of the chapters or sections in the text, and their page numbers. (You can see one at the beginning of this book.)

Consider creating a table of contents for your own writing. It can be helpful to your reader if your text is long and has many parts, as in a research report.

Before you follow the steps to using and creating a table of contents, think about these questions:

- Why is skimming the table of contents before you read a good reading strategy?
- Why can having good inquiry questions help you use a table of contents well?
- Which assignments or projects require a table of contents?

Do It Yourself

Using a Table of Contents to Find Information

- **Step 1** Before you choose books or texts, create a list of questions that you would like to answer in your research (for example, What was Stephen Leacock's first published story?).
- **Step 2** Highlight the key words and phrases in your questions (for example, What were the main **causes** of the **war** in **Bosnia**?).

How to Use and Create a Table of Contents

Steps

- **Step 3** Locate the table of contents in one of your research texts. It is usually one of the first pages of the book.
- **Step 4** Review the highlighted words and phrases in your research questions. Scan the table of contents to match your highlighted words and phrases with the chapter or section titles. If you can't find an exact match, read the titles in the table of contents to find sections that you think might have the information you need.
- **Step 5** Once you have found one or more of your target topics in the table of contents titles, use the page references in the table of contents and turn in the text to that chapter or section.
- **Step 6** Read the introduction to the chapter or section carefully. Then ask yourself: Will this chapter give me the information I need?

    If the answer is no, repeat Steps 4 and 5 to choose another chapter, or use another book.

    If the answer is yes, skim the rest of the chapter to get the main ideas. Then scan the chapter for the key words and phrases you've highlighted. When you find them, read the text around the key words carefully. Make a note of the important information you've found.

Hot tips

- Start your research with the first section in the table of contents that matches your search.
- It's not usually necessary to read an entire chapter when you are searching for specific information. You can usually find what you need in the text around the key words and phrases.

Do It Yourself

Creating a Table of Contents

Steps

- **Step 1** Decide if your report needs a table of contents. A table of contents can help guide the reader if your report is long, or includes many tables, graphs, diagrams, or illustrations.

- **Step 2** Number the pages of your completed report starting with your first page of written text. (Don't number the title page or cover page.) Include numbers on pages of diagrams, charts, and illustrations, your list of works cited, and your index, if included.

- **Step 3** Create a rough draft of your table of contents. Use the model on page 15 as your framework. What are the main headings in your work? Are there subsections with enough information that they need a subheading of their own? List all headings and subheadings that you think need to be part of the table of contents.

- **Step 4** Review the headings and subheadings that you want to include. Be sure the subheadings are listed under the correct main heading. Check that you have noted the page numbers accurately. Be sure everything is spelled correctly.

- **Step 5** Create a final draft of your table of contents.

- **Step 6** Insert the table of contents between the title page and page one of your report.

HOT tips

- Create your table of contents after your report is completely finished. You want to be sure that the content and the order of the material are final.

Shirin has just finished her final draft of a research report on changes in occupations over the last 100 years. This is her table of contents.

Model

Table of Contents

	Page
Introduction	1
Jobs at the Turn of the 20th Century: An Agricultural Society	1
Major Employers in 1900 (Pie Chart)	2
Farm Worker with Horse and Plough (photo)	2
Airplanes and Weapons: World War I	3
Billy Bishop: Flying Ace (photo)	4
The Move to Cities: The 1920s Boom	5
The Growth of the Automotive Industry (line graph)	6
The Great Depression of the 30's: Massive Unemployment	7
Waiting for the Dole: Unemployment Line (photo)	9
Women Join the Workforce: Second World War	10
The Post-War Baby Boom: Prosperity	11
The High-Tech Revolution: New Jobs	13
Canada's High-Tech Cities (bar graph)	15
Workers of the 21st Century: What Employers Want	16
Old Skills vs. New Skills (comparison chart)	17
Conclusion	18
Works Cited	19

Think about It

Use the information in the table of contents to identify the main ideas that Shirin will develop and explain in her report. Choose one of Shirin's main ideas, and predict what you think she will explain in that section.

Making It Work: Literature Studies and Reading

Use the Anthology

The report "Analyzing the "Tween" Market" (pages 80-97) includes a table of contents. What are the main sections of the report?

Activities

1. Examine the table of contents in this text, *Making It Work 12*. Explain how it is organized.

2. Use the table of contents in this text to find out where you would learn how to create your own portfolio for an interview.

How to Use and Create an Index

Before You Start

The index is an organizing feature in a text that helps you find information. The index is located at the end of the text, and helps you to locate specific words, phrases, and names that are included in the text. The index lists all words alphabetically, and lists the exact page upon which you'll find the word, name, or phrase. (You will find an index at the back of this book.) Using an index can help you find specific information quickly and easily.

Before you follow the steps to using an index, think about these questions:
- What types of texts do you read that have an index?
- Why is it helpful to be able to find information in a text quickly?
- Why is it helpful to create an index in a publication?

Do It Yourself

Using an Index in a Text to Find Information

- **Step 1** Create a list of questions that you would like to answer through your research (for example, What was the title of the first novel ever published in Canada?).
- **Step 2** Highlight the key words and phrases in your questions. Make a list of synonyms (words that mean the same thing) for the key words and phrases you have identified.
- **Step 3** Locate the index at the back of the text you're using for research.
- **Step 4** Choose a key word or phrase to look for in the index.
- **Step 5** Use the alphabetical listing order of the index to locate the key word or phrase.
- **Step 6** If you can't find that word or phrase in the index, try looking for one of its synonyms. If that doesn't work, choose another of your key words and search the index for it.

Making It Work: Literature Studies and Reading

- **Step 7** When you find the key word, use the page reference given in the index and turn to the page of the text that contains that word. Scan the page for the key word. When you find it, read the text around the key word to locate the information you need. Make a note of the information on your research outline.
- **Step 8** If you can't find any of your key words or phrases in the index, find another research text and repeat the process.

Do It Yourself

Creating an Index

Steps

- **Step 1** Carefully reread a draft version of your report. As you read, highlight the specialized words, phrases, and names that are important in your report.
- **Step 2** List your highlighted key words and, beside each, record the page number in your report on which it can be found.
- **Step 3** Put the words in alphabetical order, with their page numbers beside each. Some words may be listed more than once. Edit so that each word appears once with all the relevant page numbers in order beside it. Use the model on the next page to help you see how an index is organized.
- **Step 4** Add a title to your page: usually "Index" is all you need.
- **Step 5** Make your index the last page of your finished report.

Hot tips

- When highlighting words in your report, highlight only the ones that are specific to your topic. These are the words that readers will seek in your index. You don't need to highlight common words and phrases that you might find in many things that you read.

This is part of an index from a government publication about job resources. What do you notice about how the index is organized?

Model

A

Aboriginal Business Canada 82
Aboriginal Education and Opportunities Manual 110
Africa
    doctoral fieldwork aid 30
    internships 203, 207, 209
    work and intercultural projects 203, 207, 209

B

Biotech Career Kit 48
Bourses pour francophones 6
Business, youth
    advice/assistance 82, 83, 84, 85, 86, 88, 90, 92, 93
    awards 94
    export assistance 86, 87
    funding to hire 88

C

Cable Telecommunications Research Fellowship Program 8
cadets, Canadian 112
Campus WorkLink 99
Canada-Australia Intra- and Partner Company Training Program 129

from YouthLink, 4th Edition,
Human Resources Development Canada

Think about It

Both a table of contents and an index help you to find information. When would you use each one? Write your ideas or discuss this with a partner.

Use the Anthology

Choose any three selections from *Moving On*. Read them and list in your reading response journal the words from those selections that you think should be included in an index. Create an alphabetized index using those words and the correct page numbers.

Activities

1. Locate the index at the back of this book. Use what you know about how an index works to find instructions for revising a covering letter for a job application.

2. Think about a large project, report, or research assignment that you're working on right now. Would it help the reader if you created an index for it? If so, use the steps in this section to create one.

How to Identify Design Elements in Text

Before You Start

Authors and designers of informational texts often use special design features to draw the reader's attention to parts of the text or to important details and ideas. This is especially true of publications that want to reach a large number of readers; they have to catch a reader's interest and keep it.

Design elements take lines of print and turn them into blocks of print that stand out because of colour, shape, arrangement, size, or font style. A good design makes a reader interested in reading and emphasizes important ideas or sections. A design also has to please the reader's eye.

Before you follow the steps to identifying and using design elements to help you read, think about these questions:
- What is the first thing that catches your eye in a newspaper?
- What is the first thing that catches your eye in a magazine?
- How can understanding elements of design help you when you are asked to read information in the workplace?

Do It Yourself

Step 1 Choose a piece of text from a magazine or newspaper, or analyze one that your teacher assigns.

Step 2 Consider the different elements of design, some of which are described below:

- The **font** is the typeface or style of letters used for the print. Designers will choose a specific font to match the purpose they have for the text. For example, designers might choose an unusual font to catch the reader's eye in a small section of text. They would choose a plain font if there is quite a lot of text that must be read and understood.

- Designers might choose to change the **font size**. They may make some lines of text larger than others to emphasize key ideas. Often, titles and headings are printed in larger font size than the surrounding text.
- The **font style** refers to whether the print appears as plain, *italic,* or **bold** text. Italics are often used for the names of books and other publications, titles of films or plays, or for foreign words. Designers use bold print to emphasize words, phrases, and sections of text.
- Designers will use **colour** in specific ways to draw the reader's attention to aspects of the print or to keep the reader's interest. Titles or individual words or phrases may appear in a different colour than the rest of the text. Sometimes a coloured background will be chosen to highlight sections of the text or a whole page of text.
- Different types of informational texts use different **text arrangements**. For example, print in newspapers and some magazines or journals is arranged in columns.
- Designers might choose to put a **border** around certain blocks or sections of text and to **shade** the background. In magazines, this is sometimes done to highlight extra information not included in the feature article.
- Designers also think about the space that has no words or visuals. This is called **white space**, and it gives the reader's eye room to pause. A lot of white space makes the page clean and easy to read.
- Often, **hyphens** or **numbers** are used in front of text to help the reader understand complex information.
- Designers may be particularly creative with headings, using what is called **display type**. Display type may be set in different styles, directions, shapes, and colours.

Step 3 Note what your eye is first drawn to on the page. Identify the design element that caused you to look there.

Step 4 Examine the titles and headings/subheadings. How are font, colour, size, and word shape used effectively?

Step 5 What design features are used in the body of the text? What do they help the reader understand, and how?

How to Identify Design Elements in Text

- **Step 6** How are the blocks of information presented on the page? What purpose does each block serve? Which are the most important ones? How do you know?
- **Step 7** Critically examine the page design. What do you think was the writer's purpose in writing? How did the design help to achieve the purpose? Did the design take away from the writer's purpose at all? How?

Look at this magazine page. What first catches your eye?

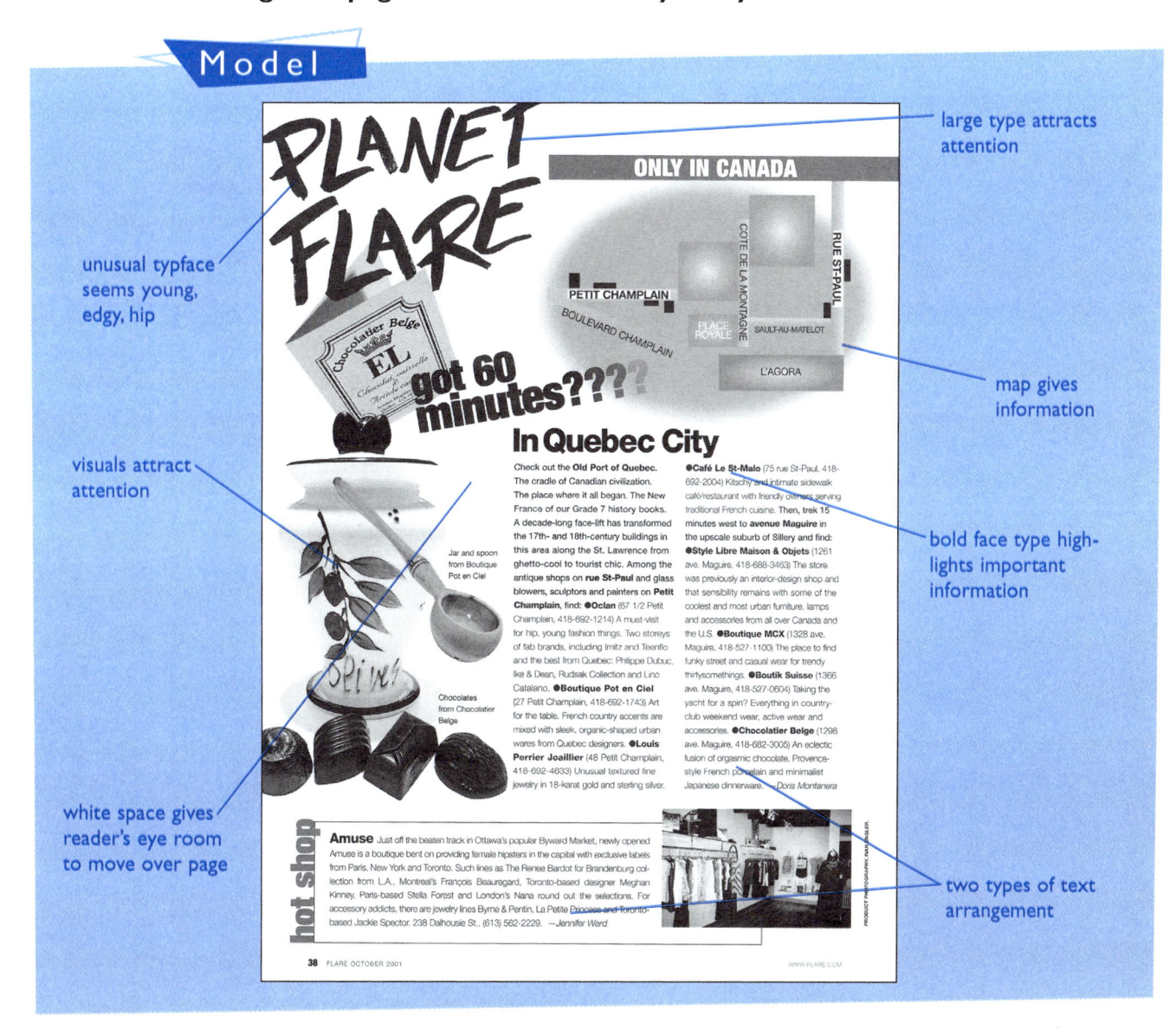

Model

- large type attracts attention
- unusual typeface seems young, edgy, hip
- map gives information
- visuals attract attention
- bold face type highlights important information
- white space gives reader's eye room to move over page
- two types of text arrangement

Think about It

What design element helps draw your eye to where you looked first? What other effective design elements do you see on the page? Why do you think they are effective?

Use the Anthology

Read "Government of Canada Services for You" (pages 233-239). What do the designers want you to see first? How does the design help draw your eye there?

Activities

1. Go to the Web site "Canada's Youth Employment Information" (http://jeunesse.gc.ca/healsafe_e.html). Using the text beneath the heading "Are You in Danger?" design a brochure to inform your peers about their safety rights and responsibilities on the job. Apply what you know about the design elements of text to produce an eye-catching and effective brochure.

2. Choose a page of this handbook to examine. Identify the design elements on the page and explain the effect of these design choices on the reader.

3. Examine two magazines supplied by your teacher. With a partner or in a small group, compare the approach to design taken by each magazine.

How to Read Visuals in Informational Text

Before You Start

Authors of informational texts will often use visuals, such as graphs, charts, diagrams, and illustrations, to help the reader understand the information they want to convey. Graphs are often used to show sets of data or numbers, so that the reader can see what the numbers mean. Graphs are usually labelled as Figures and are numbered in order throughout the text. Other visuals, such as photographs, digital images, or drawings, make key ideas stand out or get an emotional reaction from a reader. These are usually labelled Illustrations and are numbered in order throughout the text.

Before you follow the steps to reading the visuals in a text, think about these questions:
- Do you often notice that you read the visuals in a piece of text first? Why do you think this is so?
- What information do you expect to get from visuals?

Do It Yourself

Understanding Graphs and Other Visuals in Informational Text

> **Step 1** Before you can understand the visuals in a text, you need to know what those visuals are. Here is a list of some common visuals:
>
> ### Graphs
> There are three basic types of graphs. Each one shows numbers and data in a different way:
>
> - **Pie** or **circle graphs** (see page 30) divide a circle into slices of different sizes to help the reader picture the size of one set of numbers compared to another. The whole pie represents 100 percent, or the total number of what has been measured. Each of the slices represents a portion of 100 percent of the pie. Pie graphs work well if there are

only a few sets of numbers to represent. Sometimes, a legend below the pie graph will give more information about the slices of the pie.

- **Line graphs** show how a quantity of something changes over time (for example, increase in sales of DVD players since they were first introduced). You can recognize a line graph by the fact that a line (sometimes more than one) is being used to represent numbers on the graph. If there is more than one line on the graph, the lines are usually different colours, or one is a solid line while the other is a broken line.

- **Bar graphs** (see page 29) use bars or columns to represent different sets of numbers. They are used when there are many categories of information to represent. Bar graphs can be vertical or horizontal. Usually bars represent categories of information. For example, a bar graph can illustrate the proportion of workers in each occupation at a place of work. There may be a bar to represent each different type of occupation. The length or height of the bar on the graph may reflect the percentage or number of people who work at that job in the place the study was done.

  Bars can be divided into smaller parts to show different characteristics of that category. In the example above, each bar might be divided to show the number of males and females in each occupation. Each part of the bar might be a different colour.

- **Charts** or **tables** usually organize information into labelled columns. Charts and tables can include numbers and other types of information.

Diagrams are line drawings of an item or process. They are labelled to help the reader identify all the parts and how they work together. Diagrams may include a numbered legend, or explanation.

- **Step 2** Read the title and the first paragraph of the text carefully. Ask yourself: What is the author's purpose in writing this piece? What do I expect to find out? What is my purpose for reading this?

- **Step 3** Before you read the whole piece, skim it to locate the main visuals. How many main visuals are there? How many different types of visuals are there? Do they have anything in common? What will these help you to understand?

- **Step 4** Read the main visuals on the page before you read the rest of the text. This can help you focus on what the author thinks is important.
- **Step 5** Find the legend, or explanation, of each visual. (If there is a legend, it is usually just below or above the visual.) Most of the time the legend will be labelled as a figure and numbered, for example, Figure 17.
- **Step 6** Examine the visual carefully.

  - What questions does the visual answer?
  - If it is a graph, ask yourself what kind of graph it is and what kind of data it represents.
  - If it is a chart or table, examine the headings or column labels to identify the key ideas.
  - If it is a diagram, locate the legend at the bottom, and match the numbers or letters on the diagram to the names in the legend.
  - If it is an illustration or photograph, read the caption to gain more information.
  - Note questions that you have about the visual (for example, The graph gives percentages, but what numbers do these represent?).

- **Step 7** Scan the page to locate the reference to the visual in the text. Read that chunk of text carefully. It will help you to understand the general information contained in the visual. Look for the answers to the questions you asked yourself about the visual. Go back to the visual to find important details.
- **Step 8** Read the whole page of text, and use what you know from the visual to help you to understand what you read.

HOT tips

- When you examine the visual, ask yourself questions about it. Write down the questions. Look at all parts of the visual carefully. Answer as many of your questions as you can by interpreting the information it gives you.
- Look in the printed text for answers that the visual doesn't give you.

Here are some figures, from a Web site, about employment patterns in Ontario. Why do you think different kinds of key visuals are used to show information?

Model

Overview of Ontario's Employment Patterns

Introduction

Making career decisions is challenging. Making one that is "right" for you depends on finding the right information on things you need to know. On the one hand, you need to know which occupations would best suit your interests and aptitudes. On the other hand, you need information about such things as the nature of the job, future work opportunities, and education and training expectations. Career choices can be especially challenging in today's fast-paced labour market where demand for different skills seems to change quickly, with new types of occupations appearing quickly as others disappear. Understanding the labour market is an important source toward making "informed" choices.

The purpose of this overview is to provide background information on industry and occupational employment trends in Ontario. It starts with a brief description of the key factors that determine industry and occupational employment patterns over time.

Did you know that in 1999, 5.7 million people were working in Ontario. Of which...

54% were male workers	46% were female
82% worked full-time	18% worked part-time
84% were employees	16% were self-employed

Source: Statistics Canada, Labour Force Survey

First, we take a look at Ontario's employment characteristics by industry. Ontario has a diverse mix of industries, and each with a unique occupational make-up. As industries grow and change, there are corresponding changes in their occupational composition.

Next, we take a look at emerging and evolving occupations. Emerging occupations and changes in existing occupations have important implications for changing the skill and educational requirements of tomorrow's work place.

Finally, we look at expected future trends in the distribution of new job creation across industry sectors and by occupational groups to the year 2005.

What are the job trends to 2005?

Figure 7 (below) shows the percent contribution of projected new jobs created between 2000 and 2005 by occupation.

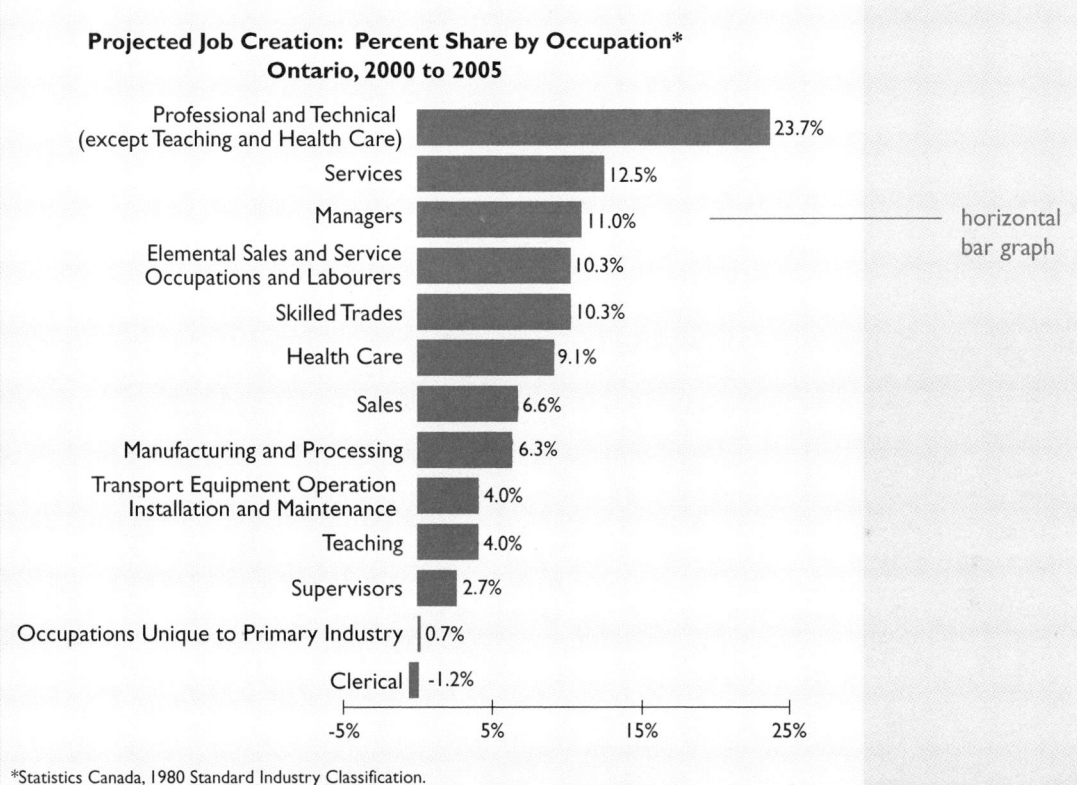

Projected Job Creation: Percent Share by Occupation*
Ontario, 2000 to 2005

Occupation	Percent
Professional and Technical (except Teaching and Health Care)	23.7%
Services	12.5%
Managers	11.0%
Elemental Sales and Service Occupations and Labourers	10.3%
Skilled Trades	10.3%
Health Care	9.1%
Sales	6.6%
Manufacturing and Processing	6.3%
Transport Equipment Operation Installation and Maintenance	4.0%
Teaching	4.0%
Supervisors	2.7%
Occupations Unique to Primary Industry	0.7%
Clerical	-1.2%

— horizontal bar graph

*Statistics Canada, 1980 Standard Industry Classification.
Source: Forecast using Informetrica's Macroeconomic Models, Canadian Occupational Projection System (COPS), February, 2000.

Clearly, most new job creation will be in occupations requiring considerable education and training. Management skills that are usually acquired through experience following a period of formal education and training will account for almost 11 percent of all new jobs. Occupations requiring a university degree will account for 25 percent of projected new jobs and those with extensive post-secondary, but less than university, degree requirements will account for 29 percent of new jobs. The smallest contribution to new jobs — 10 percent — will come from occupations that require only short, on-the-job training without a secondary school diploma.

Making It Work: Literature Studies and Reading

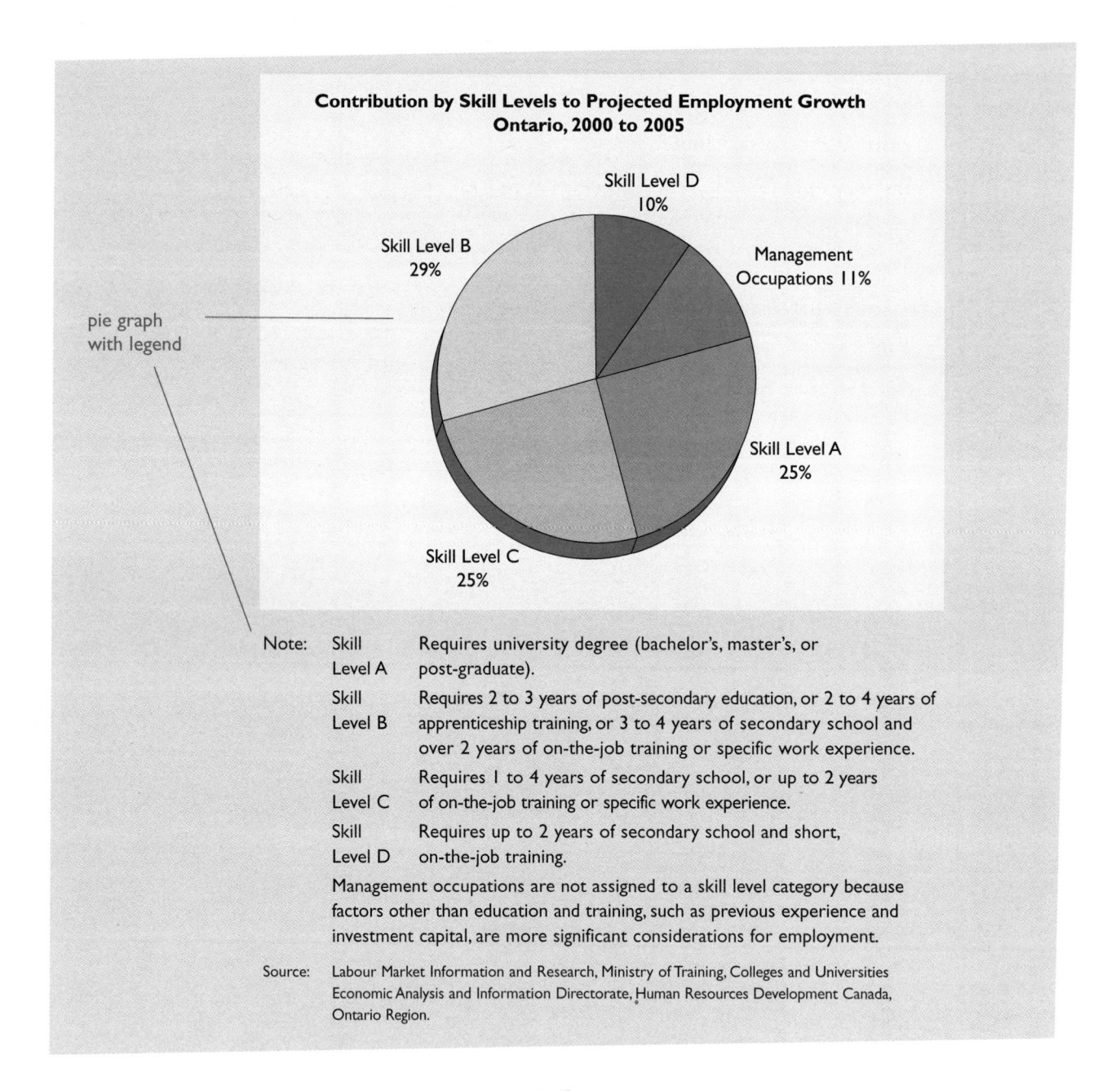

Contribution by Skill Levels to Projected Employment Growth Ontario, 2000 to 2005

pie graph with legend

- Skill Level D 10%
- Management Occupations 11%
- Skill Level A 25%
- Skill Level C 25%
- Skill Level B 29%

Note:
- **Skill Level A**: Requires university degree (bachelor's, master's, or post-graduate).
- **Skill Level B**: Requires 2 to 3 years of post-secondary education, or 2 to 4 years of apprenticeship training, or 3 to 4 years of secondary school and over 2 years of on-the-job training or specific work experience.
- **Skill Level C**: Requires 1 to 4 years of secondary school, or up to 2 years of on-the-job training or specific work experience.
- **Skill Level D**: Requires up to 2 years of secondary school and short, on-the-job training.

Management occupations are not assigned to a skill level category because factors other than education and training, such as previous experience and investment capital, are more significant considerations for employment.

Source: Labour Market Information and Research, Ministry of Training, Colleges and Universities Economic Analysis and Information Directorate, Human Resources Development Canada, Ontario Region.

Think about It

Examine Figure 7 (page 29). What type of visual is it? What important ideas does the visual represent? What questions do you have that the visual doesn't answer? Where would you look for the answer? What surprises you about the information?

Use the Anthology

Look at the chart in the report "Analyzing the "Tween" Market" (pages 80-97). Explain what is effective about reading that information in a chart instead of in a paragraph.

Activities

1. What kind of visual do you think would best show the following employment data from Statistics Canada's Labour Force Survey, 1999? Explain your answer.

   In 1999, 5.7 million people were working in Ontario, of which:
   - 54% were male workers, 46% were female
   - 82% worked full-time, 18% worked part-time
   - 84% were employees, 16% were self-employed

2. a. Choose a report you have completed for one of your classes. What kinds of visuals did you use? Why did you choose them? Why did you think they would be effective in conveying information?

   b. Now look at a report you are working on for one of your classes. What visuals would be effective in this report? Why? What information would they give?

Making It Work: Literature Studies and Reading

How to Read a Business Report

Before You Start

As an employee or as a member of an organization, you may have to read and respond to a variety of business reports.

There are many types of business reports. Some are very detailed and lengthy, such as an organization's annual report or a company's formal report on specific issues important to it. Other reports are shorter, such as proposals, progress reports, or incident reports.

Before you follow the steps to reading a business report, think about these questions:

- Why is it important to know how to read a business report?
- What kind of information do you think employers share with employees in a business report?

Do It Yourself

Step 1 Understand the format of different reports. Here are two examples:

An organization's **annual report** is a document that is issued once every year. Corporations are legally required to issue an annual report to their shareholders. Other groups create annual reports to keep interested people informed.

Groups use annual reports to describe how the organization met its goals, what its aims and missions are for the future, and to give more information about the organization. Many annual reports include financial statements, as well as one or more of the following:

- financial highlights of the year
- a message from the president or chairperson, or a statement from the Board of Directors
- articles and interesting stories about the company, including illustrations and photographs

How to Read a Business Report

- a detailed financial statement, including charts and graphs
- a business report about a specific issue or problem
- the names of the company's officers and Board of Directors

Formal business reports are usually written to report on a problem that has been studied or a change that could be made. The formal report has:

- a covering letter addressing the persons who will read the report
- a title page
- an executive summary of the report giving a brief overview of the report's main ideas
- a table of contents
- an introduction
- a discussion, in which the main ideas are presented
- a conclusion
- recommendations for solving a problem or implementing a change
- references and/or a bibliography of all of the information sources for the report
- appendices containing extra information

Step 2 Know why you are reading the business report. Ask yourself:

- Why am I reading a company's annual report? What do I want to know or find out?
- Why am I reading this formal report? Does the writer need my response? Am I the one who will be making the proposed changes or fixing the problem?

Step 3 Choose a way to read the report that matches your purpose. For example:

- Skim, or read quickly, the whole report to get a sense of what it contains overall.
- Scan, or look for key words in, the report for specific information.
- While you're reading, highlight or use self-stick notes to emphasize key ideas and information.
- To help you respond to the report, make margin notes on it or on self-stick notes to draw your attention to things you disagree with, agree with, or question.

- **Step 4** Use the report's organizational features (table of contents, headings, subheadings, sections, charts, diagrams) to locate specific parts of the report that interest you most. You might read these parts first, and then return to the other parts as necessary. This is especially true when you read annual reports on line.
- **Step 5** Use visuals and graphics to help you understand key information and ideas in the report, especially the financial part of the annual report.

HOT tips

- Skim the table of contents of a business report to find the exact sections that will give you the information you need.

How to Read a Business Report | 35

This annual report appears on Amnesty International's Web site. What things do you think the organization wants Internet readers to notice?

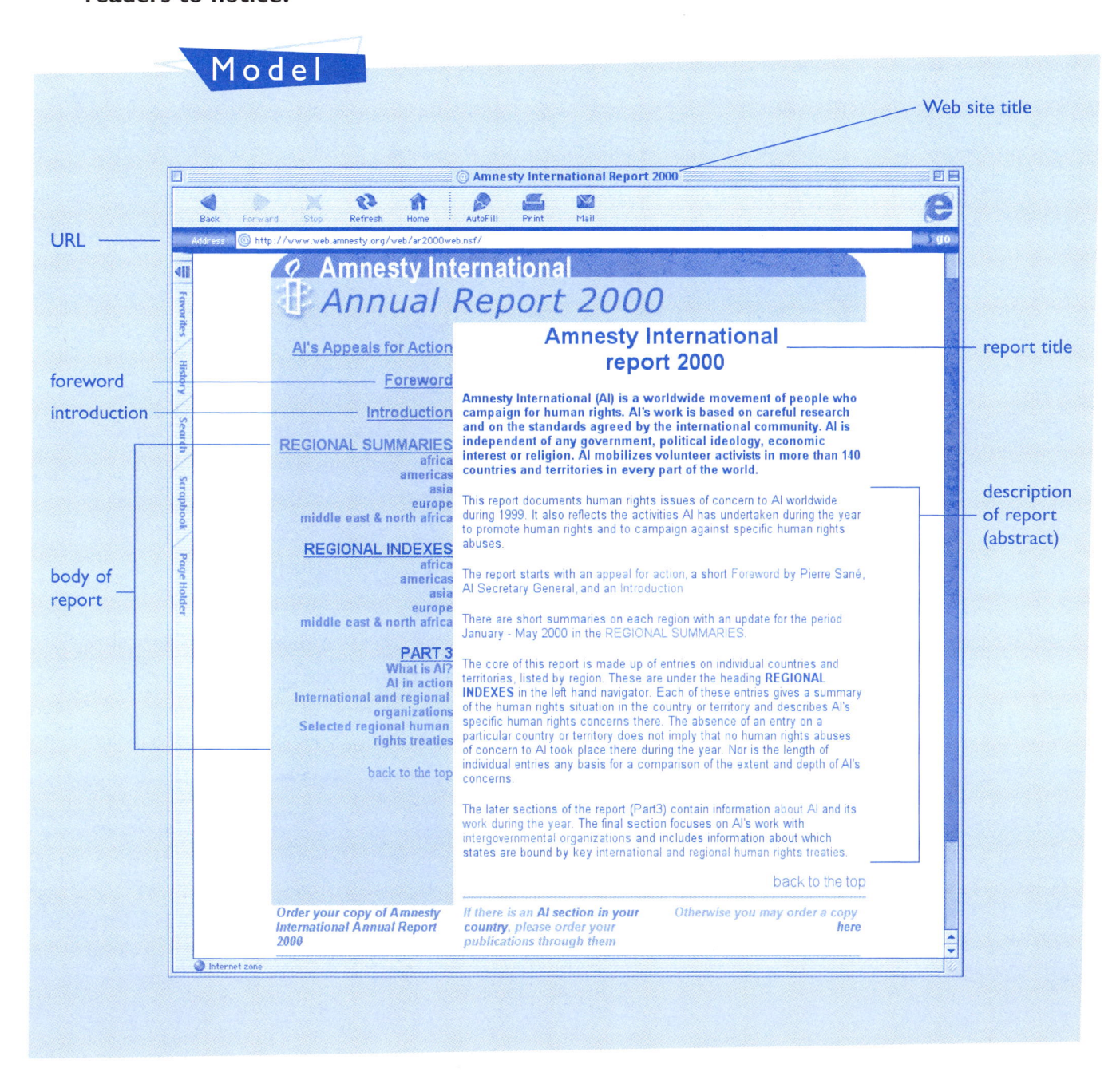

Model

Screenshot of Amnesty International Annual Report 2000 webpage with the following annotations:

- Web site title: *Amnesty International Report 2000*
- URL: http://www.web.amnesty.org/web/ar2000web.nsf/
- foreword
- introduction
- body of report
- report title: **Amnesty International report 2000**
- description of report (abstract)

Amnesty International Annual Report 2000

AI's Appeals for Action
Foreword
Introduction

REGIONAL SUMMARIES
africa
americas
asia
europe
middle east & north africa

REGIONAL INDEXES
africa
americas
asia
europe
middle east & north africa

PART 3
What is AI?
AI in action
International and regional organizations
Selected regional human rights treaties

back to the top

Amnesty International report 2000

Amnesty International (AI) is a worldwide movement of people who campaign for human rights. AI's work is based on careful research and on the standards agreed by the international community. AI is independent of any government, political ideology, economic interest or religion. AI mobilizes volunteer activists in more than 140 countries and territories in every part of the world.

This report documents human rights issues of concern to AI worldwide during 1999. It also reflects the activities AI has undertaken during the year to promote human rights and to campaign against specific human rights abuses.

The report starts with an appeal for action, a short Foreword by Pierre Sané, AI Secretary General, and an Introduction

There are short summaries on each region with an update for the period January - May 2000 in the REGIONAL SUMMARIES.

The core of this report is made up of entries on individual countries and territories, listed by region. These are under the heading REGIONAL INDEXES in the left hand navigator. Each of these entries gives a summary of the human rights situation in the country or territory and describes AI's specific human rights concerns there. The absence of an entry on a particular country or territory does not imply that no human rights abuses of concern to AI took place there during the year. Nor is the length of individual entries any basis for a comparison of the extent and depth of AI's concerns.

The later sections of the report (Part3) contain information about AI and its work during the year. The final section focuses on AI's work with intergovernmental organizations and includes information about which states are bound by key international and regional human rights treaties.

back to the top

Order your copy of Amnesty International Annual Report 2000 | If there is an AI section in your country, please order your publications through them | Otherwise you may order a copy here

Think about It

Who would read this report? Why?

Use the Anthology

Read "The Grand River Conservation Authority 2000 Annual Report" (pages 183-188). The selection in the anthology is only part of the report. What elements might you expect to find in the full report?

Activities

1. Do an Internet search to find the annual report of a non-profit organization (for example, UNICEF, Pollution Probe, The Council of Canadians, the Canadian Breast Cancer Foundation) or a for-profit organization (for example, a car company, a grocery chain, a major retailer), or obtain a copy of that organization's annual report. Examine how the report is structured and organized. Then focus on the visuals that are included in the report. What overall impression of the organization do these visuals help to create? Explain why the choice of these visuals is so important to an organization.

2. Your school is a non-profit organization. Create a design for an annual report for your school that would report information to its "shareholders" (students and parents). Make an outline of what the annual report might contain.

How to Assess and Interpret Information, Ideas, and Issues in Text

Before You Start

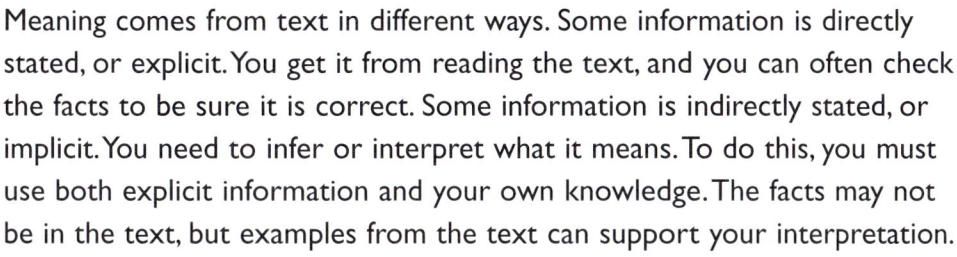

Meaning comes from text in different ways. Some information is directly stated, or explicit. You get it from reading the text, and you can often check the facts to be sure it is correct. Some information is indirectly stated, or implicit. You need to infer or interpret what it means. To do this, you must use both explicit information and your own knowledge. The facts may not be in the text, but examples from the text can support your interpretation.

Before you follow the steps to interpreting and assessing information, ideas, and issues in text, think about these questions:

- When you are asked for information that is directly stated in the text, what is a good strategy for making sure the answer you give is correct?
- Why is it helpful to discuss an interpretation with someone else?

Do It Yourself

Step 1 In order to assess and interpret information, ideas, and issues in texts, you first need to recognize the difference between explicit and implicit information in texts.

Explicit information and ideas in texts are the facts and details that are directly stated in the text. If it is listing, finding, describing, telling, retelling, or explaining what or how, it is stating explicit information.

Implicit information and ideas in texts aren't directly stated by the author. You, the reader, will need to make inferences or find the implicit ideas in the text. You are doing this if you are asking or answering questions such as the following about the information in the text:

Why did Carmel quit her job?
How did the train wreck happen?
What do you think will happen? (prediction)
Explain the underlying cause of…
On the basis of _____ (the facts and details), what can you conclude about _____?
What do you think that Trey should do?
What is the main idea? What is the theme?
What would you do if you were…?

Step 2 To assess the information, ideas, and issues in texts, ask questions about the information you've read, and note your answers. Questions might include:

- Is this information accurate? How do I know? Do I need to check these facts and details?
- Is the text current enough for my purpose, or do I need to find something more recent?
- Is this enough information, or will I have to read other sources?
- Is this the information I was looking for? Is this what I need?
- Can this source of information be trusted, or should I find another source?
- Are the ideas too limited or one-sided? Do I need to consider other points of view?
- What is my own point of view on this subject? Do I agree or disagree?

Step 3 Any interpretation you make of a text will include explicit information, as well as your own opinions, ideas, and experiences that help you understand what you have read. To support your interpretation, you need evidence from the text. You can get that evidence by noting the following:

- Does the author state clearly his/her point of view? If so, what is it? Does the point of view change? If so, tell how and why.
- If the author doesn't clearly state his/her point of view on the topic/issue, list or outline the argument or facts and details that the author does state explicitly in the text. From this, state what the author's point of view appears to be.

How to Assess and Interpret Information, Ideas, and Issues in Text | 39

- Explain how the explicit facts, details, information, and ideas of the piece lead you to your interpretation of what is the author's point of view.
- Many words that authors use have connotations, which means that we attach emotional meanings to them. Often we can see how an author feels through the words and phrases he or she uses. Note the words and phrases in the text that seem to show how an author feels about the topic. State, in general, what the author's point of view appears to be.
- Explain how the connotations of the author's words also support what you believe the author's point of view to be.
- Examine what you've written and ask yourself: Would the author agree with my interpretation?

Step 4 Write a draft of your interpretation, being sure that you have understood the facts and that you can give evidence of inferences by looking at the original text.

HOT tips

- When you're reading, ask yourself questions about the selection or the writer. Think about whether the information is new to you, whether you agree or disagree with it, and what facts you might like to check.
- Think about whether the writer's tone agrees with the writer's ideas. If not, the writer may be using irony. Read *Making It Work 12*: How to Recognize Allusion and Irony (pages 57-61) to learn how to assess such information.

The following excerpt from the novel *Bottom Drawer* is the transcript of an interview between a psychiatrist and the stepfather of the main character in the novel. What kind of information (explicit or implicit) do you think you will get about the stepfather in this transcript? Explain.

Model

Transcription
Dr. Margaret F. Cheung
Interview with Mr. Malcolm Clifton
Stepfather of Kuper, Mackenzie Ross
Case No. 101-221-9
24 September

Start

There is nothing as far as I can tell which accounts for Mac's actions over the last couple of months. He doesn't do drugs . . . believe me, I would know . . . I know what to look for and what the signs are. He's not got any girl problems as far as I know . . . in fact, he sees a girl and he runs in the opposite direction . . . the kid's far too shy and introverted for my liking . . . not that I don't like him. I like him just fine — he does his chores, keeps his nose clean, and isn't a troublemaker by any description. Once or twice maybe we've been eye-to-eye over a problem but he's always made the right decisions.

. . . well, by the right decision I mean that he gets the message that he can't operate in his own little world 24 hours a day and that he has a family he has to respond to and live with. Now Kathy tends to be too soft on him but Mac knows that he isn't going to get anywhere by trying to play the two of us off against each other. And that's basically what happened . . . a couple of times. Remember that Mac is not my real son and it has been very difficult for him to think of me as a father and I don't mind admitting that I don't get a lot of love out of that boy. To be frank with you, Dr. Cheung, I think he tolerates me like you would something that isn't going to go away. And it's been tough because I have made . . . and I keep making . . . opportunities for us to get together and build a better relationship, but . . . I guess you could say that we have a pretty good working relationship at the moment, but that's as far as it goes. He may see it differently and I don't know how

use of the word "I" tells reader what the stepfather thinks

he'd describe it because as I say Mac is not a talker. He gets going on that computer of his and he's lost in cyberspace...

...cyberspace? Waste of space, I call it. TV wasn't bad enough, they had to create another way to rot their brains. I'm telling you, it was nearly over my dead body when we bought him that computer set-up, but Kathy insisted that was what he wanted and... well, hell, I s'pose I was doing my best at that time to be "Dad" and let him know that we wanted the best for him. It's been a waste of time really because that computer is like a magnet and it just draws him away from the family and into his own little world. He should be out meeting girls and making friends.

Oh, he plays sports all right. He's good enough not to ride the pine but he could be something special if he'd just concentrate and work on his basics. I can count on one hand the number of times that we played a little one-on-one in the driveway. You give him a bump, make it a little tough for him to get by, and he just stomps off. No shouting, no swearing, no anger, he just puts down the ball and wanders off. I've been trying to change that, but sometimes I just have to give up. He's so hard to reach.

explicit information about how Mac acts with his stepfather in a given situation

Mac is not crazy. Not crazy as I know crazy to be. He's too quiet, too withdrawn, but he's not crazy. And you have to be crazy to want to kill yourself, doctor.

Mac is different, he doesn't have any reasons; he's just fog-bound and working on foggier if you ask me. I know we aren't supposed to hit kids these days and I've never laid a hand on Mac, but sometimes I think that maybe a couple of belts across the ass would make him wake up and smell the coffee. That's the biggest problem with half of these ear-ringed, pony-tailed, pampered teenagers who look more like girls than boys... and the other half of them expect to be treated like adults without having to earn it. I work for my money, always have, always will, and if Mac's got a softer life growing up than I did, well that's just fine, but if I'm

implicit information; tone tells reader how stepfather feels about teens

paying for it there has to be some accountability. Some basics and some rules, that's all I ask. Now I'm sorry but I do have to go. I have a daughter who needs time with her daddy because this whole thing has not been a good experience for her . . . and that reminds me, Kathy says that you want to interview Keelie as well . . .

Think about It

Was your prediction about the kind of information you would get correct? What implicit information did you get about Malcolm and his relationship with Mac? Give evidence from the text to support your interpretation.

Use the Anthology

Read "Mother to Son" (page 109). Read between the lines of this poem. Imagine what the son said to the mother that gave her a reason to share what she says in the poem.

Activities

1. Think of a topic you'd like to explore. Using key words to aid you in your search, access three Web sites that contain information about your topic. Assess the accuracy of the information on each Web site by finding out something about the sponsors or creators of the site. Check the dates posted on the Web site. How recently was the information updated?

2. Search the newspaper for stories and articles about a current issue, whether global, national, or local. Choose one story and one opinion piece about the issue. Read each one and list the explicit information. Then think about what ideas or information are implied but not stated directly. List these. Finally, write a brief opinion paragraph explaining your personal thoughts about the issue. Use facts and details from what you've read.

How to Recognize the Perspectives of Authors and Readers

Before You Start

We all have values, or things we believe are right, and beliefs. Our values and beliefs come from our experiences in life, and help to shape our perspective, or how we look at life. Writers bring their perspectives to their writing, influencing what they tell us and how they tell it.

When we share an author's perspective, we may understand his or her ideas easily. When we don't share an author's perspective, we may have trouble understanding his or her ideas.

In fiction, you may learn the author's perspective by understanding the theme, since authors often reveal truths about life that they themselves believe. When you are reading a text for information, you need to ask yourself who is writing the text and to what degree you can believe the ideas. This is especially important when you are reading texts on the Internet.

Before you follow the steps to recognizing perspective, think about these questions:

- What kinds of texts do you like to read? Do you think they are written from a similar or different perspective to your own?
- Why is it important to understand another person's perspective in the workplace?

Do It Yourself

Create a Diagram to Define Your Perspective

> **Step 1** Create a diagram of circles that will help you define how your experiences influence your understanding of texts. Draw a small circle, about 5 cm in

Steps

diameter, on a piece of paper. Inside it, write your name and your date of birth. Draw a circle around it. Write your gender and your current age inside it. Draw another circle around it. List the names of your parents or guardians, and any siblings, inside it. Draw another circle around it. Inside it, list the names of your extended family — grandparents, aunts, uncles, cousins, and so on.

Step 2 Continue your diagram with circles to represent the communities that you are part of. Around your extended family circle, draw a circle to represent your cultural community. Here, list details about your cultural heritage, language, and religion. Include any significant descriptive words that you think are appropriate, including names of friends from this cultural community.

Your next circle around the others represents the geographic community where you live (your neighbourhood, municipality, township, or reserve). In this circle, describe where you live and the school that you attend. Include the names of your friends who are outside of your cultural community but attend your school or live in your community.

Your next circle represents the region of Canada where you live. Describe what living here is like for you.

The last circle represents Canada. In this space, describe what it is like living in Canada, and what living in Canada means to you.

Step 3 Look at your completed diagram. Choose the two circles you think have had the most influence on you. Explain in a short paragraph how these have influenced your values and beliefs.

Step 4 Looking at the entire graphic, write a paragraph that summarizes your unique perspective — your values and beliefs. You may organize the ideas in the paragraph in any way you wish: from the inside to the outside circle, or in order of their importance to you in your life.

How to Recognize the Perspectives of Authors and Readers | 45

HOT tips

- When you read, keep your circle diagram in front of you. It will remind you of your perspective on the world, and the reasons why you might agree or disagree with the ideas and opinions of others.

Do It Yourself

Recognizing the Author's Perspective in Literature

- **Step 1** Choose a selection to read, or read one assigned by your teacher. Identify the theme (see How to Understand Themes in Literature, pages 62-68). The themes that authors reveal can reflect the author's own beliefs and perspective.

- **Step 2** Conduct research into the life of that author. Since, like yourself, authors live in communities that have shaped their values, you might discover a writer's perspective by doing research about him or her. (Finding biographical information is just one way to try to understand an author's perspective. Sometimes this information is not relevant, and does not help you understand the perspective.) You might choose to read a biography to learn about an author's life or details about the time when he or she lived. Or you might check your literature text for biographical information about an author. Consider creating a diagram for the author like the one you created to define your own perspective.

- **Step 3** Compare what you know about an author's life and times with aspects of your own life. How are you similar? How are you different? Despite the differences, what can you appreciate about the author's point of view?

- **Step 4** Use your notes to write a few sentences that state what you think the author's perspective is. Do you think the author necessarily always writes from that perspective?

Do It Yourself

Recognizing the Author's Perspective in Informational Texts

Steps

- **Step 1** If you're reading a textbook or a scholarly work on a subject, check the book (usually at the front) for information about the author. Many publishers give background information about the author that establishes the author's connection to the field of study. Does it inspire you to trust the author?

- **Step 2** If you're reading an editorial, essay, or opinion piece on a topic, try to keep an open mind about the ideas and information you're reading. Read it a second time. Note the ideas and information that you think might be questionable or that you don't agree with. (See also How to Assess and Interpret Information, Ideas, and Issues in Text, pages 37-42).

- **Step 3** Find some background on the author of the piece. Sometimes, when the author is writing in the first person, you'll learn important details from the author in the text itself. A publication might give information about the author, such as any positions held in organizations. This information can give you an idea about the author's expertise in a field. On the Internet, sponsors of home pages will tell you something about themselves that will help you decide if their information is reliable or trustworthy. Ask yourself: What is the author's perspective? What have I discovered about the author that might explain his/her perspective?

- **Step 4** Think about your own perspective on the topic or issue. Write about it and explain why you hold that opinion. What points of the author's do you agree with? Where do you disagree with the author? Identify anything you think is still unclear about the topic.

- **Step 5** Try to see the issue or question from the author's point of view. Ask yourself, "If I were the author, how would I see this differently?"

- **Step 6** Re-examine your own point of view or perspective on the question or issue. Modify your ideas in light of what you've read.

How to Recognize the Perspectives of Authors and Readers

> **HOT tips**
> • Before you read, take time to consider what you know, think, and believe about the topic of your reading. This will help you to identify the ways in which you might agree or disagree with an author.

The following is an excerpt about writing from someone else's point of view. What is your own opinion on this topic? Why do you think as you do?

Model

Whose Story to Tell?

by Josie C. Auger

Throughout American literary history, writers have used a romanticized image of Native people in order to enhance their country's identity as a colonizing nation. As a result the depiction of Aboriginal peoples in novels and newspapers has often been negative.

But today, Native people are no longer depicted as savages, but as people with a rich culture. Still, there are problems. Recently (in my English class at the University of Alberta) the subject of cultural appropriation came up. Initially, the non-Native students thought it was alright for them to write about the spirituality of Native people. However, the Native students taking the course felt it was wrong to write about spirituality—based on the fact Native people have been depicted so negatively.

[writer tells reader the setting she comes from — university]

I opposed non-Native people telling our stories for two reasons: firstly, the cultural ceremonies that Native people conduct are sacred. Certain Elders have stipulated that in order to keep the culture sacred it should not be written about. Secondly, Native writers should be given more opportunities to have their stories published— to earn a living and to help the individual and the community.

[author's stated perspective]

[author identifies herself as Native — "our"]

[author states number of reasons and offers support]

What I have learned is that it's difficult for whites to understand why Native people are angry and hurt when others write about them.

> I realize the dominant society does not comprehend the disastrous effect colonization has had on Native people. As well, I know there are a number of non-Native people who feel guilty about what has happened in the past. They wish to change the present in order to shape the future.
>
> One white female student, responding to a <u>question from the professor</u>, said some people feel a need to appropriate Native culture because it's a trend, and there are many people who are disillusioned with their own religion and are searching for something different. When some of my non-Native classmates agreed there was nothing wrong with appropriating Native culture, the hair on the back of my neck stood up. I sensed a conflict.

— author is not the professor, but a student in the class

Think about It

What is the author's point of view? Support your answer with at least two details from the model.

Use the Anthology

Read "Why We Crave Horror Movies" (pages 22-25). Why might a reader trust Stephen King's viewpoint in his essay? How is his perspective on horror different from the perspective of other writers on the topic?

Activities

1. Choose a topic to write about which seems popular among the public right now. Write an opinion piece about the topic. Include details about yourself in the piece to give the reader a sense of your own perspective on the topic.

2. Consider a fiction text you are reading right now, or a movie you have just seen. Ask yourself: From which character's point of view have I experienced the story? Then think about the story again from the point of view of another character. In a series of paragraphs, retell the story from the point of view of this other character.

How to Analyze the Role of Suspense

Before You Start

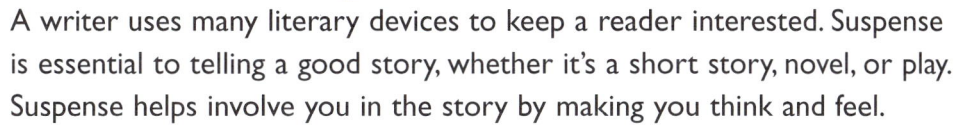

A writer uses many literary devices to keep a reader interested. Suspense is essential to telling a good story, whether it's a short story, novel, or play. Suspense helps involve you in the story by making you think and feel.

Suspense is a feeling of being tense or nervous when an unknown or threatening force grips a character we care about in a story. It starts with a feeling that something is going to happen, then builds as the events unfold. The action reaches a high point, or climax. Some turning point is reached, and then the tension eases. Sometimes suspense builds because we don't know *what* will happen. Sometimes suspense builds because we don't know *when* something will happen.

Before you follow the steps to analyzing suspense in text, think about these questions:
- What things do you remember most about stories that you read?
- Do you enjoy tension in a story when you read? Explain.

Do It Yourself

Steps

- **Step 1** As you read a suspenseful story for the first time, try to notice when you become more tense, when you have reached the story's high point, and when you begin to relax.

- **Step 2** Read the story a second time. This time, highlight or note several points in the story (use self-stick notes if it's not your own text copy): when the suspense starts, what events build the tension, and when it reaches its peak.

- **Step 3** Take a look at the sections you have highlighted. Complete a plot graph (see Line Master 1, available from your teacher) to create a visual representation of the story's suspense pattern.

- **Step 4** After you've completed these steps, reflect by asking yourself: What role did suspense play in making this an effective story? How did it help me to understand the characters and the conflict?

This excerpt is from *The Boy in the Burning House*, a novel by Tim Wynne-Jones. Note in your reading response journal where you feel the suspense building.

Model

Jim looked into Ruth Rose's eyes — moss green they were — to see if she was crazy, too. She stared right back at him without a flicker. Maybe there were different kinds of craziness.

"I'm here," she said, "because of that Fisher-man. He may have married my mother, but he will never be my father. If we're going to work together you'd better get that through your teeny skull."

"Work together?"

"Just listen!" she said. Her hands had curled into fists, and Jim didn't doubt she would use them. He swallowed, listened.

"Fisher is a murderer," she said.

Jim snapped his head back as if, with a lightning sucker punch, she had hit him.

"What?"

"You heard me." Her voice was all breathy now. She looked around as if Father Fisher might be in the field somewhere. Then she returned her gaze to Jim, her green eyes flashing. "And you're going to help me put him away."

It was obvious now she was crazy. Jim shook his head in disbelief and turned to go.

"Don't move," she said. Jim froze. She walked around him, blocking his path. She was a head taller than he was and bristling with wiry strength.

"That's better," she said. She blew the hair off her face. "You don't really know anything about him. You probably don't even know that his name actually is Father. Even my mom calls him Father, which is gross."

Jim tried to speak as gently as he could, not wanting to disturb her any more than she already was.

"I'm sorry," he said. "But this doesn't have anything to do with me."

She went on as if she hadn't heard. "When he became a pastor, he got his name legally changed to Father. He used to be Eldon, Eldon Fisher. Do you know what a fisher is?"

"Like Christ, a fisher of souls —"

"Wrooong! I mean the animal."

"Like a weasel!" said Jim.

"Worse," said Ruth Rose. "More like a wolverine."

"Yeah." Jim had seen a fisher that a trapper caught. And he remembered what the trapper had called it. "A killing machine," he said.

Ruth Rose nodded appreciatively. "Do you know how a fisher kills a porcupine, Jim? It hides up in the tree where the porcupine lives and when the porkie comes home in the morning and heads out to its branch to sleep, the fisher drops down in front of it from the branch above. The porcupine can't turn around — the branch is too small — so it can't defend itself with its tail. And then do you know what?" She stepped right up to Jim as if she were the fisher and he were the porcupine. "The fisher bites the porcupine's face off."

Jim tensed. Then he relaxed a bit and rolled his eyes.

"You think I'm an idiot, don't you?" she said. "Go on, say it."

"You're an idiot," said Jim. Then she shoved him so hard he tumbled right over and before he could move she was standing over him.

"He got his name changed to Father, all legal and everything. Just like he legally adopted me when he married my mom. He likes to make things look neat and tidy. You know why? Because he's got a lot to hide."

Jim flinched. September nights came on quickly and here he was, far from home, gabbing with a lunatic.

"I've got to go," he said, edging upwards to a sitting position. When she didn't pounce, he clambered to his feet.

"Don't you want to hear who he murdered?" she said.

Jim shook his head. "No, thank you." He started walking away, didn't look back.

"I'll tell your mother," she shouted after him. "About your tree jumping." He didn't stop. Those days were behind him.

"I need your help, Jim," she said. "You need somebody's help," he muttered to himself. He glanced back to see if she'd heard. He had only walked twenty paces or so, but he could hardly see her. In her black clothing, she was lost in the shadow of the pine tree. Now that he had opened some distance between them, he felt a little sorry for her.

"I'm sorry I can't help," he shouted.

"You will be," she hollered back at him.

He shuddered at the fury in her voice, but was far enough away by now to laugh to himself at her threat.

He was heading down the hill towards the creek which flowed by as sly as a rumour, when she called out to him again. He looked up and she was standing above him at the lip of the hill, silhouetted against the light — dark and mysterious like a cut-out.

"Jim Hawkins," she shouted, trying to catch her breath. "Fisher killed your father."

Think about It

Would you want to continue reading the novel at this point? Why or why not?

Use the Anthology

Read "In My Hands" (pages 34-47). Work with a partner to find the suspenseful moments. Discuss whether there are more suspenseful moments in a true story than in a work of fiction.

Activities

1. Use the plot graph on Line Master 1 to record the suspense patterns in a television drama. Describe what happens on the plot graph just before commercials.
2. Compare the suspense patterns of different kinds of stories or films (for example, compare a mystery story to a horror story.) What seems similar? What seems different?

How to Analyze the Role of Description

Before You Start

Description is the technique of using details and images that appeal to our senses to make all elements of a story seem real to the reader. By choosing just the right words and phrases to describe characters, setting, and conflict, writers help readers see what they want them to see. Effective description might make readers:

- see something clearly in all of its colours and shades of light
- see something differently
- focus on something or someone they might have missed or ignored
- feel an emotion
- remember a similar time or place
- understand a character or another person
- feel the action
- understand a different point of view

Before you follow the steps to analyzing description in text, think about these questions:

- What things do you remember most about stories that you read?
- What types of events might you need to describe to a co-worker, employer, or employee while at work?

Do It Yourself

Step 1 Choose a descriptive paragraph to read or read one that your teacher has assigned. The first time you read it, try to gain an overall impression.

Step 2 Read the paragraph a second time, this time noting the words and phrases that describe and give detail. Record different kinds of describing words (for example, words of colour, words of motion or action, words that describe feelings or emotions, words that make you see, hear, taste, touch, smell) using different colours of pen for each or note them under different headings in a chart in your notebook.

Steps

- **Step 3** Try reading the passage aloud to a partner, but skip the words you've noted. Now read the passage again, this time with the words you've noted. Ask your partner: Which one was easier to understand? Why?

- **Step 4** Re-examine your list of words. What colour of pen is most noticeable? Which heading has the longest list? What is it that the writer most wants you to picture or sense in this passage?

- **Step 5** Using what you've noted, explain the important role description plays in the piece you've just read. (You may wish to refer to the discussion of effective description in Before You Start.)

Hot tips

- Offer the reader the right amount of description. Too much detail will overwhelm your reader.
- Use simple but vivid words.

This excerpt is from *The Boy in the Burning House*, a novel by Tim Wynne-Jones. What descriptive words do you notice right away?

Model

He stared at the girl. He could be wrong. If it was her, she had changed, got herself some breasts and an attitude. She was all in black from her sneakers to her dark-and-stormy-night hair. It was inky black, from a bottle, he guessed. Even her lips were black. She had a gold nose ring. She looked tough as nails. And yet there was something sweet — a scent of roses — which was how he remembered her name.

"Ruth Rose," he said.

"Bzzzz!" she buzzed like a bee. "A hundred points for Jim Hawkins who pisses on scarecrows."

Think about It

Examine the words and phrases that the author uses to describe Ruth Rose. What types of descriptions are they? Are they effective? Why or why not?

Use the Anthology

Read "I Know Why the Caged Bird Sings" (pages 176-181). There are a number of striking descriptive contrasts in this excerpt. Focus on how the author describes her first attempt to apply for a job at the Market Street Railway Company. Compare what she says with how she really feels. Which words or phrases do you think are most effective? Why?

Activities

1. To practise describing, do a "Five-Minute Observation." Focus your attention on a particular person, object, or scene. Brainstorm every detail you can to describe it. Then arrange the details into sentences and paragraphs.

2. Examine a paragraph, longer prose work, or poem you have written. Highlight overused words, or words that you think hold little meaning. Use a thesaurus to find more effective words, and substitute them for the ones you've highlighted. Read both drafts to a partner, then choose the most effective words for your final draft.

How to Recognize Allusion and Irony

> Before You Start

In every job, people use certain tools to do their work well. The tools that writers use are literary devices. Writers use them to craft and shape language so that it is powerful, rich, and clear. Two literary devices are allusion and irony.

Allusions are references that writers make in their writing to specific events, people, and things. These references are not explained to the reader, because they don't have to be: the writers know their audience and believe their readers will be familiar with most of the references. Allusions allow a writer and a reader to know that they share an unspoken understanding of meaning.

Irony is at work when there are two levels of meaning present in a text: what appears on the surface to be true — and what is really true. There are three types of irony:

— *Verbal irony*, or sarcasm, occurs when what a person says is the opposite of what he or she means (for example, a goalie lets in an easy goal, and a fan shouts "Nice save!").

— *Dramatic irony* occurs when the reader knows something important that the characters don't know. This can create comedy (if the characters who don't know appear ridiculous) or suspense (if the audience is waiting for something serious that they suspect will happen to the character).

— *Situational irony* occurs when the outcome of a situation is the opposite of what the reader or audience expects.

Before you follow the steps to recognizing allusion and irony in texts, think about these questions:

- Why do you think irony is inappropriate in texts that you might read in the workplace?
- Why would allusion work well with a group of people who are all in the same line of work?

Do It Yourself

Recognizing Allusion

- **Step 1** Many allusions are to people or places. Look for capitalized words and phrases in the text. Use self-stick notes to highlight these when you find them.
- **Step 2** Some allusions are to historical or current events. Use self-stick notes to highlight any descriptions of these events when you find them.

    Test whether the things you've highlighted are allusions by asking yourself the question: Does the writer give an explanation or background information for the reference, or not? If no explanation or background is given, it's an allusion, because the writer assumes you already know the information.
- **Step 3** Next, ask yourself: Am I familiar with this allusion, or not?

    If you are not, then continue to read that section of text. Sometimes you'll find clues that will tell you what the allusion means.
- **Step 4** Is the allusion a key to understanding the writer's point? If not, read on and return to it later. If so, do some quick research to get the information you need.

HOT tips

- If you find an allusion that is unclear, place a self-stick note to mark it. When you are finished reading, research it or ask someone to explain it.

Do It Yourself

Recognizing Irony

- **Step 1** Choose a text to read or read one assigned by your teacher. Predict what you think the piece will be about based on the title and what you learn from the first paragraph. State your prediction clearly in your reading response journal.

Steps

- **Step 2** Read the text. Pay close attention to your own reactions as you read. When what you read *sounds* right but starts to *feel* wrong, it's possible that the writer is being ironic: he or she might be saying one thing, and meaning another.
- **Step 3** Keep reading the text for signs that the writer's meaning is different from what it seems on the surface.
- **Step 4** Re-examine your expectations about the topic of the piece. Ask yourself: Would most other readers have the same expectations? Why? List the details that led to your expectations to see how they differ from the tone.
- **Step 5** Writers sometimes use irony to show readers that we should change our perspectives or see something in a different light. Ask yourself: Is that what the writer is doing in this piece? If so, what is the different perspective he or she wants us to see?

Hot tips

- If the author's tone doesn't match the ideas, the author may be using irony.
- Read the title of the selection. What ideas do you expect to find in the text? If the ideas don't match your expectations, the author may be using irony.

Read the title of this excerpt. What kinds of allusions do you expect to find based on the title?

Model 1

What TV Does to Kids

by Harry Waters

His first polysyllabic utterance was "Bradybunch." He learned to spell Sugar Smacks before his own name. Recently, he tried to karate-chop his younger sister after she broke his Six Million Dollar Man bionic transport station (she retaliated by bashing him with her Cher doll). His nursery-school teacher reports that he is passive, noncreative, and has almost no attention span; in short, he is very much like his classmates. This fall, he will officially reach the age of reason and begin his formal education. His parents are beginning to discuss their apprehensions — when they are not too busy watching television.

Think about It

Identify all of the allusions that are made in this passage. What helped you identify them?

Why might the title of the following text be ironic?

Model 2

Man, You're a Great Player

by Gary Lautens

Occasionally I run into sports figures at cocktail parties, on the street, or on their way to the bank.

"Nice game the other night," I said to an old hockey-player pal.

"Think so?" he replied.

"You've come a long way since I knew you as a junior."

"How's that?"

"Well, you high-stick better for one thing — and I think the way you clutch sweaters is really superb. You may be the best in the league."

He blushed modestly. "For a time," I confessed, "I never thought you'd get the hang of it."

"It wasn't easy," he confided. "It took practice and encouragement. You know, something like spearing doesn't come naturally. It has to be developed."

"I'm not inclined to flattery but, in my book, you've got it made. You're a dirty player."

"Stop kidding."

"No, no," I insisted. "I'm not trying to butter you up. I mean it. When you broke in there were flashes of dirty play — but you weren't consistent. That's the difference between a dirty player and merely a colourful one."

"I wish my father were alive to hear you say that," he said quietly. "He would have been proud."

Think about It

When did the piece begin to feel wrong to you? Identify the exact point in the piece when you got the sense that the writer believes something quite different from what he says. What specific things from the text convinced you that there was a different meaning? What type of irony is this? (Refer to Before You Start to review the three types.) Explain how you know.

Use the Anthology

Read the first line of "The Interview" (page 165). Then, when you've read the whole poem, explain to a partner why that line is ironic.

Activities

1. Watch a suspense film, and look for situations in which you, the viewer, know something that the actors or characters do not. Write a brief paragraph to explain the importance of dramatic irony in suspense films.
2. Rewrite the paragraph from "What TV Does to Kids" (page 59) to include more up-to-date allusions. Then read it to a partner. Discuss the effect of your more current allusions on the reader.
3. Read an article from a current newspaper or magazine. Identify the allusions it contains. Then rewrite part of the article for a different audience, such as someone your age who lives in another country and experiences a different culture. Which allusions will you have to explain? Why?

How to Understand Themes in Literature

Before You Start

Explaining the theme is one of the most challenging parts of reading literature. A theme is an insight about life that an author wants the reader to know.

In an information text, such as an essay, article, or report, the theme is fairly clear. The author wants to give you direct information. But in fiction or poetry, authors almost never state their theme directly. They want you to read the piece and experience the message they want to share. A theme is often something true about life or about human nature that you learn from the characters' experiences. In short fiction or poetry, writers usually explore one theme. In longer works, such as novels or long plays, there may be many themes.

Before you follow the steps to finding themes in literature, think about these questions:

- What are some things that you think are true about life?
- What are some things that you think are true about human nature?
- How can understanding things about life and human nature help you when you work with others?

Do It Yourself

Finding the Theme in Short Prose Fiction or a Play

- **Step 1** Choose a piece of short fiction or a play, or read one that your teacher has assigned. Read the whole piece from the beginning to the end in one sitting.

- **Step 2** Consider carefully what you think and feel about the story or play. Write your thoughts and feelings in your reading response journal. Your responses will give you important clues to the theme. You might reflect on questions such as the following:

  - What strikes you as being true to life about the story?
  - What specific situations or people does the story remind you of?

How to Understand Themes in Literature

- What does the story remind you of in your own life?
- What advice did you find yourself giving the main character(s)?
- Would you make the same choices as the characters in the story? Why or why not?

Step 3 Think about the main topic of the story or play. State it in one sentence (For example, This story was about a man who kept a secret from his family.). This is not the theme of the story, because it doesn't state a truth about life or human nature, but it will help to bring you closer to stating the theme.

Step 4 Focus on the conflict in the story or play. Write notes to answer these questions:

- What was the main character's biggest problem?
- Who or what was the cause?
- What factors or forces in the story or play made the conflict hard to solve? What characters made the conflict hard to solve?
- Why was it important to the character to solve the conflict?
- How was the conflict solved?
- How will the main character's life change as a result?
- Do you think this is a conflict that many people experience?
- Would most people react the same way to the conflict that these characters do?

Step 5 Ask yourself: What knowledge and understanding have I gained about myself, human nature, or human beings from the way the characters act in the story? State your ideas in one sentence (for example, I learned from the story that people may keep secrets because they want to protect others).

Step 6 Ask yourself: What did I learn about life from the story? State your ideas in one sentence (for example, I learned from the story that life often asks us to make hard choices, and that we can't think only of ourselves when we make them. We have to think about the other people who can be affected.).

Step 7 Reread the title of the text. Does it fit with one of your statements (for example, Since the title of the story is "Necessary Lies," I think the theme is that sometimes in life we have to hide the truth, even if we don't want to, in order to protect others from harm.)?

Step 8 Read your notes, and then write a statement that tells the theme of the short story or play.

Making It Work: Literature Studies and Reading

HOT tips
- When you're trying to decide on, and think about, the theme in a story, it can be useful to start by considering the conflict.
- To find the theme in a poem that tells a story (called a narrative poem), use the steps for finding the theme in short fiction.

Do It Yourself

Finding the Theme of a Poem

Steps

- **Step 1** Read the whole poem from beginning to end, at least three times. Read the poem aloud at least once to hear the words the poet uses.

- **Step 2** Respond to the poem in your reading response journal. Ask yourself: What did the poem make me feel? Make me see? Make me hear? Make me think of? What did I like about it? What confused me about it?

- **Step 3** What does the title tell you about the subject or topic of the poem? Write a statement to answer the question.

- **Step 4** Examine what is literally happening in the poem. Record your answers to these questions: Who is speaking? Where is the speaker? What is happening? What is the speaker thinking about? What feelings does the speaker describe?

- **Step 5** Which words are repeated in the poem? How does repetition influence the meaning of the poem? Take notes to answer these questions.

- **Step 6** There are lots of words that writers use to represent ideas. These words are called symbols (for example, roses = beauty; flying = freedom; sun = life). Which words in the poem have symbolic significance? How do these give the poem a deeper meaning? What might that deeper meaning be? Answer these questions in your reading response journal.

- **Step 7** Try to fit your thoughts and feelings about the poem into these statements:

  > This poem is about _____ and it makes the reader see/feel/hear _____.
  > The poet might be saying _____ about _____ (topic) because _____.

- **Step 8** Turn your statements above into one statement that expresses the theme of the poem.

Here is a piece of short fiction. What kinds of words can help you figure out the theme?

Model

Judgement Day

by Jack C. Haldeman II

They were coming.

I woke up knowing that, just as I knew they wouldn't take me. There are many things in my life I am ashamed of. They might take Laura, though. She's the one truly good person I know. I nudged her awake.

"I had the strangest dream," she said, sleepily brushing the hair from her face.

"I know," I said. "I had it too."

She looked at me with that half-awake way that she has. I could tell she understood.

"They won't take me either," she said. There was sadness in her voice.

"They might. You've never hurt anyone in your life. You're a kind and good person."

She shook her head. "I'm not good enough," she said. "Not for them."

It was true and we both knew it in our hearts. They wanted perfection, nothing less.

Laura shivered and I held her close. The bedroom was dark and we shared a secret the whole world knew. I listened to the clock tick. There wasn't much to say. We stayed that way all morning and I didn't go to work.

Everything stopped that day. No wars, no work, no play: it wasn't a day for that. Men and women around the world looked to the stars and into their hearts. They saw the darkness, the shortcomings. Each in their own way grieved for what man had become. It had to come to this; all the promise, all the hopes. There was nothing to do but wait. They were coming.

The dream had a billion voices and it touched us all. The powerful and the poor got the same message. When night had passed we all understood. They wanted the best.

It was fair, no one could dispute that. They weren't interested in the ones who held power, or the wisest, or the richest people in the world. They wanted the best the Earth had to offer. Nothing less would do. In the night they touched our minds they had also made their decision. There was nothing to do but wait for them to come and see who they had chosen.

It wouldn't be the smoothest talker who would speak for Earth. The wisest men wouldn't plead our case before the collective minds of a thousand planets. They weren't interested in words or great deeds; what they wanted was kindness and compassion and I wondered where they'd find it.

They were giving us the best chance that Earth could have. There would be no deceit, no lies, no misunderstandings. They would take two — they had chosen two — and they would speak for Earth. There would be no others, there would be no second chance. We waited and wondered.

Everything stood still. Even the pulpits were quiet. What we had seen that night had made us look deep into our souls and we all fell short. We looked at what we could have been and measured it against what we had become. It was a dark pain and we all felt it. Then they came.

They came in a silver ship and said nothing. There was nothing to say, they had said it all that night. Silently they went to those they had chosen and then they left.

They took to the stars two dolphins, a mated pair.

We are waiting for their decision.

Think about It

If this story were to really happen, do you think that people you know would react in the same way that the characters do in the story? Why? What might that tell you about human nature?

Use the Anthology

Choose three or four pieces of fiction or poetry from *Moving On*. Using the title as a clue, think about what the subject of each piece will be. Do any of the titles give you a good clue as to their theme? Discuss your answers with your class.

Activities

1. Use the Step-by-Step instructions (page 62) to help you find the theme of a short story or play you've been assigned to read.
2. Use the Step-by-Step instructions (page 64) to help you find the theme of a poem you've been assigned to read.
3. Explain the similarities and differences in finding the theme of a poem as compared to finding the theme in other types of fiction.

Writing

TABLE OF CONTENTS

Exploring Writing	70
How to Write a Letter	74
How to Write a Memorandum	78
How to Create an Action Plan	81
How to Develop and Implement a Research Plan	85
How to Revise a Draft	89
How to Write a Short Essay	95
How to Cite Sources	100
How to Prepare a Portfolio	106
How to Write Instructions	111
How to Write a Report for the Workplace	115
How to Write a Poem	120

Exploring Writing

Writing can take many forms, from lists and short notes to timetables, essays, and job applications. Some kinds of writing have specific formats; others can be set up in several ways. Each format also has its own conventions, or ways that language is used. Answer these questions in your reading response journal to learn where your writing is already strong, and how you can improve it.

Personal Writing Inventory

1. When do you write?
2. How often do you write letters, résumés, and so on?
3. How often do you use e-mail?
4. When you hand in writing, or read it aloud, in class, what comments do you usually get?
5. What do your answers tell you about yourself as a writer?

▸ The stages of the writing process

Writing is not instant for anyone. Writing is a process. To write well, you need to take time, you need a place to write, and you need someone to read what you have written, which can include yourself. You may need several drafts before you are happy with your product.

These are the stages of the writing process. You don't need to follow the stages in order. Use them any time during your writing to help you come up with ideas, think about your writing, and make your writing better.

Thinking and/or Talking
⬇
Prewriting
⬇
Drafting
⬇
Revising
⬇
Publishing

Thinking and/or talking

You are the best judge of what you need to do to write. Some people need to think for a while about a topic before writing about it. Others need to talk, draw, role-play, or explore their ideas with others. Use whichever method best helps you prepare to write.

Making It Work: Writing

Prewriting

In the prewriting stage, decide on these elements of your writing:

the topic

the purpose

the audience

the format

Next, explore your topic by writing everything you know about it, or rereading your journal for ideas of how you think and feel about certain issues.

Gather information on your tFopic through brainstorming, webbing, researching, mapping, and/or interviewing. When you are satisfied with the points you have written down, outline them by organizing them into an effective order.

Drafting

Produce your first draft in the format you chose. Put your ideas down on paper, following your outline. Double-space so that you have room on the page to revise your work. Consider using a computer to help make revisions easier. Focus on your ideas now, and make corrections to your writing style later.

Revising

Revise your work for content. Ask: Am I happy with the information that I have included? If you are not happy with the content, begin your writing again. If you are satistfed with what you have written, read over your work to be sure it says what you want it to say. See if you put emphasis in the right place, if the organization is effective, and if your points are accurate, specific, and clear.

Next, revise the style. Check your spelling, grammar, and punctuation. If you are using a computer, use spell check and grammar check to help you. These functions may not support Canadian Standard English and will not highlight the different uses of words such as *know/no*, or *there/their/they're*. Be sure to do a manual check of your spelling and grammar as well. Use a directory to check that addresses and names are correct. Share your work with a peer who can add comments and criticisms. (See pages 84-94, How to Revise a Draft, for additional suggestions.)

Publishing

Publish your final product. Check to see that your piece — whether it's a memo, a report, a letter, or an essay — follows the conventions for that format of writing. See How to Cite Sources, pages 100-105, for information on how to list any sources that you have used. Present your work to its intended audience, by handing it in or distributing, posting, or performing it.

How to Write a Letter

Before You Start

Letters to a business, school, or employer are formal letters. They use formal language, and have a particular format (see models, pages 76 and 77). Letters or notes to friends or family are informal. These letters may use informal language or slang, and don't have to be in a specific format.

Types of formal letters include:

— a **covering letter:** to accompany a résumé when applying for a job
— a **letter of acceptance**: to confirm an offer of employment
— a **declining letter**: to reject an job offer of employment
— a **letter of agreement**: to outline briefly to an employee the conditions of a job
— a **letter of recommendation**: to offer support for skills, knowledge, and attitude toward work from a teacher, mentor, or former boss
— a **thank-you letter**: to offer thanks for a gift, a thoughtful gesture, a job interview

Before you follow the steps to write a letter, think about the following questions:

- What letters have you written recently? Do you think they were clear and direct?
- What do the letters that you have seen look like?
- When and why might you have to write a letter?

Do It Yourself

Step 1 Figure out your purpose, audience, topic, and format. You will need to keep these variables in mind as you write. For instance, if your audience is a potential employer and your format is a covering letter, you will need to use a formal tone.

Steps

- **Step 2** Brainstorm the facts you want to include in your letter.
- **Step 3** Put your facts in the best order. Delete anything unnecessary or repetitious.
- **Step 4** Draft your letter. Start with the recipient's name. Your introductory paragraph should state your purpose and may include a heading. The body should have two to three paragraphs that explain why you are writing and/or what you want. The concluding paragraph should be brief and effective, summarizing your purpose and possibly outlining a next step.
- **Step 5** Revise your work. Check your content and organization. Edit your grammar, spelling, and punctuation. Make sure names and addresses are correct. Read your letter from the recipient's point of view. If your letter is particularly important, ask a mentor and a peer to edit it.
- **Step 6** When you are happy with your letter, type it (if you haven't yet). For a formal letter, put your address at the top, followed by the recipient's address. Format your letter so there is a good balance of white space and room for your signature (see model on page 76). If you are writing an informal letter or a thank-you letter, you can write it by hand neatly instead of typing it.
- **Step 7** Send your letter by regular mail, electronic mail, or fax, or deliver it in person.

Hot tips

- To get started, you might want to work with a partner and role-play a scene (trying to return a pair of jeans at a store for a refund, interviewing someone for a job). Use the ideas, feelings, and words of the scene to help you write your letter.
- Try not to begin too many sentences in your letter with the word "I."
- Use a letter as a record-keeping device (for example, as confirmation of an important phone call).
- Revise your letter by reading it aloud to a peer. Does it make sense to you? To your listener? Make any suggested changes.

Making It Work: Writing

Here are two letters. Why is the language different in each one?

Model 1

letter set in block style, with all information beginning at the left, and each new kind of information set in its own "block" of print

addresses —
Joan Albert
123 Ontario Street
Peterborough, Ontario
N2M 1X8

phone number — (705) 555-4567

e-mail address — Joanalbe@hotletter.com

date — April 29, 2002

Viola Sussex
Art Gallery Director
345 Blockline Avenue
Peterborough, Ontario
N3X 2M2

formal greeting — Dear Mrs. Sussex:

subject line — Re: Position opening at art gallery

introduction — I enjoyed meeting you at my job interview last Tuesday. Thank you very much for making the time to see me.

purpose of letter — I have not heard from you since our interview, so I thought I would send this quick note. The time I spent working at the art gallery in Curve Lake gave me a great deal of experience handling many tasks during busy times, and I think I could be a real asset to your staff.

details

For your convenience, I am attaching another copy of my résumé. I look forward to hearing from you.

formal closing — Sincerely,

signature in blue or black pen — *Joan Albert*
Joan Albert

Model 2

informal greeting — Hi Winston:

introduction — I'll never go on another blind date again. What were you thinking when you set me up with your friend Lin? We have nothing in common. She is five years older than me, lives out of town, likes classical music, and hates computers. Could anyone be more different? We had a terrible time last night. Don't ever set me up with anyone again. *— details*

informal closing — You were wrong on this one, but I'll still meet you tonight for the game.

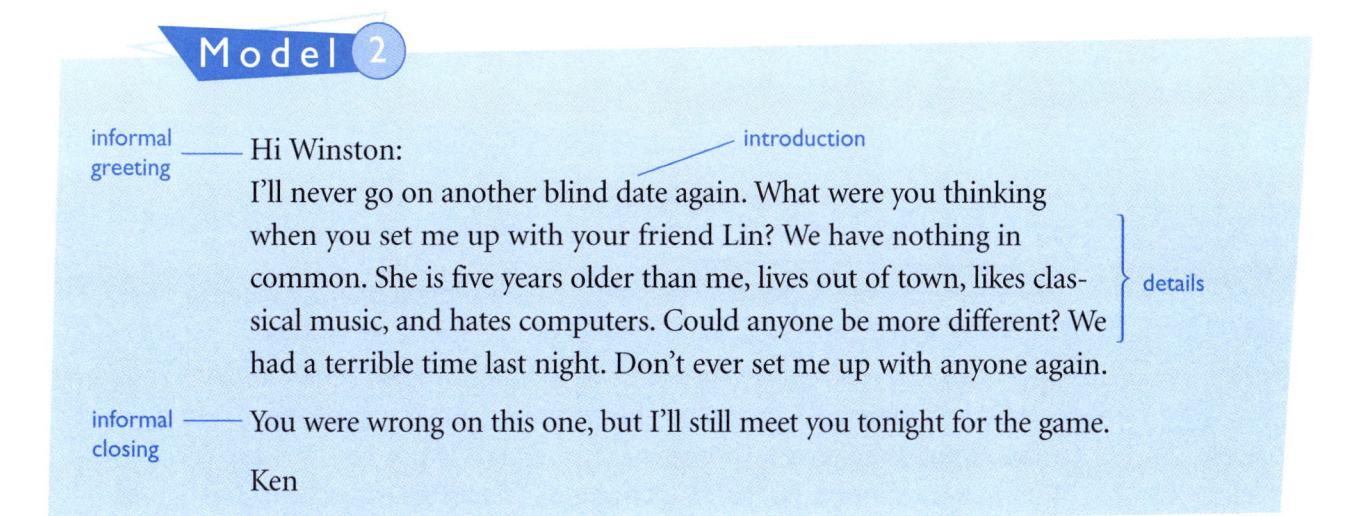

Ken

Think about It

What are the two purposes of the letter on page 76? What makes each of the model letters effective?

Use the Anthology

Read "Childhood, 1916" (pages 129-133). Explain whether you think using the letters is an effective way to tell a story.

Activities

1. Write a letter to a mentor, teacher, or former employer requesting a letter of reference.

2. Write a covering letter, to accompany a résumé, for a job advertised in the newspaper. Indicate why you're the best person for the job and why you want it. Don't repeat what is in your résumé — just highlight the key points.

3. Write a thank-you letter to a relative for a birthday gift or to a friend for a thoughtful gesture.

4. Write an e-mail letter. Give only necessary information, and don't be inappropriate. Avoid overusing all-capitals (this indicates yelling). Choose an appropriate subject, and indicate the subject at the top of the letter. Use some e-mail characters, or emoticons, to get your points across: :-) for a smile/ ;-) for a wink/ :-(for disappointment.

How to Write a Memorandum

Before You Start

A memorandum (usually called a memo) is a short letter written to a co-worker or supervisor and is the most frequent form of work correspondence. (Ask your teacher or an office administrator for a memo that you can read as a sample.) A memo can be posted or e-mailed. It's designed to be read quickly, and requests or provides information. Memos can be used as covering letters for reports, claims, announcements, adjustments, orders, sales figures, greetings, records of agreement, telephone follow-ups, and proposals.

Before you follow the steps to write a memo, think about the following questions:
- What kind of information would you want to share with a number of people at work very quickly?
- Why is it important to read a memo carefully?
- How can the ability to write a good memo help you in the workplace?

Do It Yourself

Steps

- **Step 1** Set up page by listing Date, To, and From and fill in the information. (Refer to the model on page 79.)
- **Step 2** Add Subject to the list and describe it. Be specific and concise. If the subject needs to be dealt with immediately, indicate its importance.
- **Step 3** In your first paragraph, indicate what the reader needs to do, such as answer a question, act on information, make a decision, call a meeting, read a report, or pass on information.
- **Step 4** Summarize the information, listing it from most to least important. Assume your reader does not have much time to read the memo, so keep it simple, brief, and clear. Know your audience and be professional and factual. Your tone should be persuasive and friendly.
- **Step 5** Check your content. Make sure you did not leave out any information. Will your reader be able to understand your message? Consider asking a peer to check it.
- **Step 6** Correct your spelling, grammar, usage, and punctuation.

How to Write a Memorandum | 79

HOT tips
- Memos should not include rumours, gossip, or jokes.
- Be sure the memos you write are professional and appropriate, as they may be read by many people in a workplace.

Here is a memo. How is it organized?

Model

Date: January 5, 2003
To: All Hospital Staff
From: Rose Govier, Manager, Human Resources
Subject: Staff Growth 2003, Two Department Goals

⎫ header is written in full, one item per line

Please find attached a copy of the Management plan for Staff Growth for the New Year.

As you know, 2002 was a year of familiarization with the Staff Growth plan. For 2003, the plan will be fully implemented. The plan requires each department to assess how effectively last year's goals were met and to write two new department goals for this year.

⎫ purpose is in the first paragraph with a summary of the action required

Within the next two weeks, your manager will be in touch with you to set a meeting date for your department to accomplish this task. In the meantime, please read the Management plan and begin to consider your department goals.

If you have any questions, please contact me at Extension 581.

greeting (Dear____), closing (Yours truly), and signature are never included

Think about It

Why is it effective to include lines for Date, To, From, and Subject at the top of the memo?

Use the Anthology

Read "Maternity, parental, and sickness benefits" (pages 189-193). Write a memo to request a sick leave from your employer, using the information in the brochure.

Activities

1. Write a memo to tell other students about an upcoming car wash to raise money for charity.

2. Imagine you work at a car dealership. Write a memo to your manager requesting additional information about a new model of car.

3. Write a memo to your teacher presenting an action plan for an independent study (see How to Create an Action Plan, pages 81-84).

How to Create an Action Plan

Before You Start

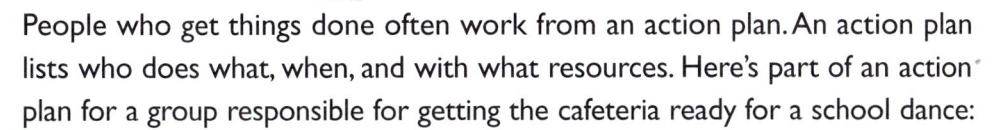

People who get things done often work from an action plan. An action plan lists who does what, when, and with what resources. Here's part of an action plan for a group responsible for getting the cafeteria ready for a school dance:

Who	What	When	Resources
Sandeep	arrange for custodial staff to move tables	Friday after school	head custodian
Mikhael	purchase decorations	Wednesday evening	committee's petty cash

Before you follow the steps to creating an action plan, think about these questions:
- In what situations at school do you think an action plan would be useful?
- In what situations at work do you think an action plan would be useful?

Do It Yourself

Steps

- **Step 1** Choose a goal for your action plan — something specific that you want to achieve, and that you think you can achieve. Write it down.
- **Step 2** Record the steps you need to take to achieve your goal. Remember to make the steps specific. Be sure that they are steps you think you can achieve.
- **Step 3** Describe and list the resources you need, including research materials, contact people, and money.
- **Step 4** Think about the time it will take to achieve each step and the total time it will take to achieve your goal. You may want to record this information on a timeline, a calendar, or a day planner.

- **Step 5** Revise the content of your plan. Make sure your steps are in an order that is useful to you, such as chronological or most important to least important. Consider highlighting the priorities.
- **Step 6** Check your grammar, spelling, and punctuation.
- **Step 7** Use columns, check marks, numbers, and headings to help you organize your information. If the action plan has an audience in addition to yourself, make sure the format looks professional.
- **Step 8** Follow your plan, updating it as you complete actions. Schedule time each week, in your calendar or agenda book, to see how well you are following your plan. If you need to, make changes or additions to any part of your plan.

Hot tips

- Make sure that you can accomplish each action in your plan. Accomplishing elements of your plan will help you to keep a positive attitude.
- List target dates for completion on your personal calendar.

The following is one way to create an action plan. What do you notice about the way it is organized?

Model

An Action Plan for Getting the Job I Want

My Goal ——————————————————— goal noted at top of plan
To get the job I want

Steps to Take to Reach My Goal

Action	Date Complete
Organize a work area	
Set aside time to work on a job search	
Get a social insurance number	

How to Create an Action Plan

chart form makes it easy to check off an action when you complete it

each step is in point form, beginning with an action verb

<u>Ask</u> a teacher, mentor, and/or former employer for a job reference	
Decide exactly what I'm looking for in a job	
Make sure the message on my answering machine sounds professional	
Look for job postings at employment agencies, in newspaper ads, on the Internet, and in the Guidance Department	
Let people know I'm looking for a job	
Make an appointment with someone in my area of interest to find out more about what the job is like (informational interview)	
Look for courses I can take and resources I can read to help me become more employable	
Complete job application forms	
Update my résumé	
Respond to appropriate ads by writing covering letters to match my résumé	
Make a phone list with all of the contacts on it	
Prepare for a job interview	
Make sure I have professional clothes for the interviews	
Write thank-you notes for the interviews	
Follow up the interviews with phone calls to the employers	
Evaluate my plan weekly to make sure it is manageable and see if anything should be changed	

column to record date that you completed an action

Resources
People, Internet, books and articles on job hunting, guidance department, newspaper ads, employment agencies

specific resources noted on plan

Think about It

Why is it effective to list the steps of an action plan in chronological order?

Use the Anthology

Read "Northern Spirit Gallery, Business Plan Executive Summary" (pages 230-232). What information does its action plan give you? Do you think the final product shows that the action plan was followed? Explain.

Activity

1. **a.** Create an action plan for completing a Web search, giving an interview, applying for a summer job, or planning for a one-day store closure for inventory checking.

   b. Share action plans with a peer. Check together that your plans are achievable and focussed.

   c. Ask someone with work experience to examine your action plan and offer advice on how to improve it.

How to Develop and Implement a Research Plan

Before You Start

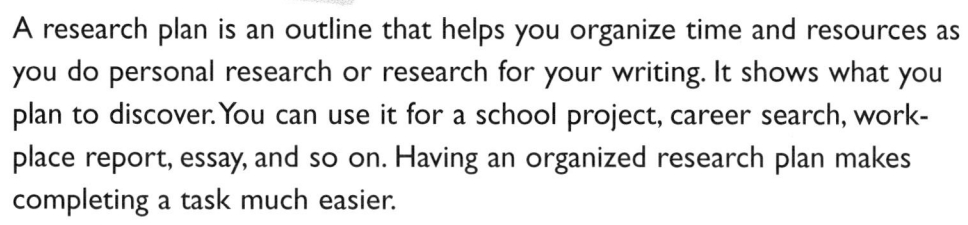

A research plan is an outline that helps you organize time and resources as you do personal research or research for your writing. It shows what you plan to discover. You can use it for a school project, career search, workplace report, essay, and so on. Having an organized research plan makes completing a task much easier.

Before you follow these steps to developing a research plan, think about the following questions:
- What is the difference between a research plan and an action plan?
- When might you need a research plan in the workplace?

Do It Yourself

- **Step 1** Choose a topic that interests you or about which you would like to learn. You might want to brainstorm a variety of research topics and then narrow your topic to a main point.

- **Step 2** Decide on the thesis of your study. Ask: What do I plan to prove or illustrate? Keep the thesis, audience, and format of your study in mind as you plan your research.

- **Step 3** Think about the best places to find information on your topic. Consider the Internet, interviews with experts, newspapers, magazines, books, and videos. For instance, for a job search, consult a database for career opportunities. Most libraries have on-line computers to help you locate material on your topic. When you find a source, use the table of contents and/or the index to locate information on your topic (see How to Use and Create a Table of Contents, pages 12-16, and How to Use and Create an Index, pages 17-20).

- **Step 4** Read your sources carefully. Think about what information will prove your main point and appeal to your audience. Formulate inquiry questions on your topic that you can answer as you research.

Making It Work: Writing

- **Step 5** Take notes which are relevant to your main point. If you use index cards, you can use one card for each idea. Then you can easily sort your cards to organize your information.

    Keep your notes clear and correct, recording quotations word for word. Put in your own words any ideas that will flesh out your study. Cite all your sources. Document all information about your sources, using a separate card for each quotation and work cited (see How to Cite Sources, pages 100-105).

- **Step 6** Analyze whether your information and ideas are sufficient, relevant, and suitable to your form and purpose. You may find that some information is unnecessary. You may also find you need to go back to a source to add details. This will be much easier if you have kept accurate notes on page numbers, authors, and titles. Reconsider your main point. Does it need to be changed at all?

- **Step 7** Sort your notes by topic. You should be able to see how the points connect. Create an outline using the information from all of your sources. The outline is a skeleton of your work. You can write it in sentences or point form. Revise it as you go until you are confident that it illustrates your thesis in the order in which you will develop your work. When you write, expand your points into paragraphs.

- **Step 8** Evaluate your research and outline again. Does everything flow and make sense? Check your grammar, punctuation, and spelling if you are handing in your research plan.

- **Step 9** Begin your assignment when you are pleased with your research plan.

HOT tips

- Make sure the information you gather is correct, particularly when you use a source from the Internet. Check when the Web site was created, how often it is updated, and who wrote it.
- A reference librarian can help you find information in your library.

Look at the headings for the following research plan. Why do you think they are an effective organizing tool?

Model

Research Plan

Name: Kareem Sami

General Topic: Finding a Job

Specific Topic: Marketing Yourself

Main Points:
1. How to present yourself
2. How to connect yourself with those already in the field

Inquiry Questions: How can you talk to people you don't know? How can you let people know about your skills? How can you keep them informed about your skills?

— inquiry questions will be answered by the research

Proposed Procedure for the Study: Talk to people in the workforce, research my topic, and write an essay

Potential Sources: guidance department at school, employment or job skills training centre, Internet, books and articles on job hunting

Title: Marketing Yourself: Presenting Yourself to People in the Workforce

Thesis: As a job-hunter you need to learn how to talk to people you don't know and convince them you would be an asset to their company.

— thesis or main point is what you want to prove

Outline:
I. Prepare to talk to people you don't know
   A. Get a list of contacts for the field you are interested in
      1. Check employment agencies, guidance department at school, Internet, and newspaper
   B. Imagine the needs of potential employers
      1. Research their Web sites, annual reports, and company newsletters

— outline is a skeleton of your work written in point form or sentences

Making It Work: Writing

outline illustrates your thesis in the order in which you will develop your work.

   C. Prepare an argument for what you can add to their company
      1. Review your résumé
      2. Review your job portfolio
      3. Practise being interviewed
II. Talk to the people in an interview
   A. Explain the skills you have to offer
      1. Show them your job portfolio
      2. Highlight examples of your skills
   B. Tell them the value you can add to the company
III. Contact them after the interview
   A. Write and send a thank-you letter for the interview
   B. Call them again
      1. Ask if they reviewed your résumé
      2. Call back after a longer period of time to update them about your skills

Conclusion: By following these steps, you will establish ongoing communication with your contacts, so they will get to know what you can offer them.

Think about It

What, if anything, would you add to this research plan?

Use the Anthology

Read "Learning to Work Safely" (pages 168-172) and the opening screen of the Young Worker Awareness Program Web Site (pages 166-167). Create a research plan on how to learn more about workplace safety.

Activities

1. Find other examples of research plans from books and Web sites. What format did you like? What was particularly helpful about the way the plans were organized?

2. Organize an independent research project on a topic of your choice using the steps and model on pages 85-88.

How to Revise a Draft

Before You Start

Before you give a final piece of writing to a teacher for assessment, or to an employer, you need to revise it, sometimes more than once. Read your work as though you were a critic, making sure the language is clear and your ideas are understandable.

Before you follow the steps for revising a draft, think about these questions:
- What do you find most enjoyable about writing?
- What do you find most challenging about writing?
- How does revising drafts help you meet your challenges?

Do It Yourself

- **Step 1** Complete your piece of writing.
- **Step 2** Give your work to a peer to check that it is clear and holds his or her attention. If you have used a computer, print your work. Use your peer's feedback where it will improve your work. Here are some questions for your peer to consider:

    - Is it interesting?
    - Do I understand it? Should anything be made more clear?
    - Is everything in the best order?
    - Are any points unnecessary, vague, or repetitious?
    - Are the introduction and conclusion effective?

- **Step 3** Add details and examples to your writing or cut unnecessary information and repetition from it where necessary. Use a different colour of ink so that your changes or additions will be easy to read.

Similarly, if you are making your comments and changes directly on your computer file and not on your printed copy, use a different colour of type or use bold or underlined text.

Here are some questions to consider when deciding whether your work is complete:

- Does your writing suit your audience?
- Does the content of your writing fit with the format you have chosen?
- If you used any researched information, does it flow naturally with your writing?
- Is your work original?
- Did you say what you wanted to say?
- Is your title appropriate?

Step 4 When you are happy with the content and how you have organized it, focus on the style. Read your writing several times. If you are using a computer, decide whether you find it easier to think about and change your work on-screen or on a printed copy. Concentrate on one or two elements with each revision. (For example, if you often have trouble varying your sentence structure, devote one reading to focussing on sentence structure. Make sure that every sentence doesn't start with a noun and a verb.)

If your teacher gave you any editing checklists, use them. Here are some other questions to consider:

- Does every word count? Tighten your writing. Make sure you didn't repeat yourself or use a number of words where one will do.
- Does your writing flow? If it doesn't, try to strengthen the connections you made between your ideas. The connection may be apparent to you, but is it to your reader? To make it flow, add linking words (for example, *furthermore, therefore, accordingly*) or transitional sentences.
- Do you have any run-on sentences or sentence fragments? If run-on sentences have been a problem for you, read your piece backwards from the final sentence to the first sentence, to see if you need to add any end punctuation.
- Is your writing in the active voice? See if your voice is consistent.
- Do your verbs agree with their subjects in number?
- Is your writing vague? Be specific.
- Is your word choice appropriate for your audience? Would a different word be more suitable?

- Is your word choice varied?
- Is your tone appropriate for your topic and audience? (For example, if you are writing an article for the school newspaper on a serious issue, you don't want to sound as though you are joking.)
- Is your use of point of view and gender consistent? (For example, in the Model, the writer consistently writes from the first-person point of view.)
- Is your language inclusive and anti-discriminatory? (For example, if possible, use the plural "they" to avoid using he or she.)
- Is your writing descriptive, vivid, and interesting?
- Does each paragraph have an introductory sentence, two to four body sentences, and a concluding sentence?

Step 5 If you have time, leave your work for a few days before revising it further. Then check the content and style again.

Step 6 If you haven't composed your work on the computer, type it on the computer now and use the spell check and grammar check to help you. The computer program won't find all spelling mistakes, so look for Canadian Standard English spellings and for words that sound the same but are spelled differently (*know* and *no; their, there,* and *they're; too, to,* and *two*). Make sure that names and addresses are spelled correctly. Use Canadian Standard English spelling consistently. Check again that you varied your punctuation and word choice.

Step 7 Publish your final draft using the format you have chosen.

HOT tips

- If you revise on a computer, you may prefer to do all of your rereading on-screen, or to print a draft and make changes on the printed copy. Do whichever works best for you. Using a printed draft can often help you see things you might not notice on-screen.
- Every piece of writing can be improved. Avoid handing in anything until it is the best you can do.

> **HOT tips**
> - When you are revising a piece of writing, pay particular attention to the writing conferences and lessons that your teacher has given recently. They are the lessons he or she will most likely consider when evaluating your work. Also, carefully consider any rubrics distributed.

Here are first, second, and third drafts of a piece of writing. What is different about each one?

Model

First Draft:

During the Christmas season I got a job at the beauty counter of a local department store. It is the busiest time of year to sell make-up. I was really busy. The make-up company I rejpresented was giving away a free gift with purchase of $30.00. The catch for the customers was that may of our items sell for $29.00, so customers had to buy two items to qualify for the free make-up pack. I sold lots of make-up. Most of the customers are regulars, so they know exactly what they want. Sometimes there were line-ups of six people waiting to be served.

your first draft may contain some errors

write all ideas

Second Draft:

Everybody can use a little extra money around Christmas time, including me. This year, to help with my Christmas expenses, I got a job at the beauty counter of a local department store. It is the busiest time of year to sell make-up. Sometimes there were line-ups of six people waiting to be served. The make-up company I represented was giving away a free gift with purchase of $30.00. The catch for the customers was that may of our items sell for $29.00, so customers had to buy two items to qualify for the free make-up pack. This policy helped me to sell lots of make-up. Selling was a lot easier than I expected it to be. Most of the customers are regulars, so

good introductory sentence; a few sentences to back it up

second draft focusses on content

they know exactly what they want. In the two weeks that I sold make-up, I had fun, made good money, and was able to use my earnings to help give my family a great Christmas.

— concluding sentence

Third Draft:

———————— check content again

Everybody can use a little extra money around Christmas time — including me. This year, to help with my Christmas expenses, I got a job at the beauty counter of a local department store. It is the busiest time of year to sell make-up. In fact, sometimes there were line-ups of six people waiting to be served. To add to the customers' incentive to buy, the make-up company I represented was giving away a free gift with a purchase of $30.00. The catch for the customers was that many of our items sell for $29.00, so they had to buy two items to qualify for the bonus. This policy helped me to sell lots of make-up, easily. Most of the customers were regulars; consequently, they knew exactly what they wanted. In the two weeks that I sold make-up, I was very busy, gave my customers what they wanted, and was able to use my earnings to help give my family a great Christmas.

focus on grammar, spelling, and punctuation

focus specifically on writing style

changes in word choice help points flow naturally

variation in punctuation and sentence structure

Think about It

Assume that the model above was part of an assignment to write an informal paragraph about a job. Were all of the changes necessary? Are there any other changes you would make?

Use the Anthology

Why would the selection "Words That Count Women In" (pages 122-127) be useful when revising a draft?

Activities

1. Look at assignments and tests you have done in the past. Focus on the teacher's corrections and comments on your writing. Make a list of problems you have had and need to pay attention to in your writing.

2. Write an essay on work experience you have had (for instance, a summer job or a volunteer position). Revise your essay, keeping in mind the steps on pages 89-91.

How to Write a Short Essay

Before You Start

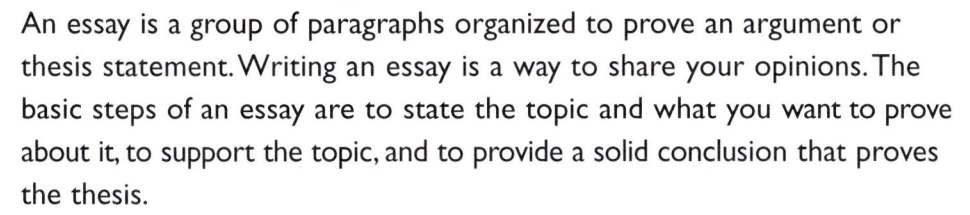

An essay is a group of paragraphs organized to prove an argument or thesis statement. Writing an essay is a way to share your opinions. The basic steps of an essay are to state the topic and what you want to prove about it, to support the topic, and to provide a solid conclusion that proves the thesis.

Most essays have three parts — an introduction, a body, and a conclusion. Here is one way to set up your essay:

The **introduction** should include several sentences that:
- catch the reader's interest
- introduce the main topic and its importance
- state the thesis, or what you plan to prove
- name the topics that will support the thesis
- link the introduction to the first body paragraph

The **body paragraphs** each support one of the topics mentioned in the introduction. Each body paragraph includes:
- a topic sentence
- specific support (examples, illustrations)
- an explanation/analysis/elaboration of why that support is significant, related directly to the thesis statement
- linked words or sentences to make ideas flow and to connect topics
- a concluding sentence

The **concluding paragraph** should contain:
- a sentence that restates the thesis
- a summary of what you have proven and why
- a concluding sentence that delivers an impact to the reader.

Before you follow the steps to write an essay, think about the following questions:
- What essays have you written recently? Do you think that you stated your point clearly?
- What would you most like to write an essay about? Why?
- What would you like to improve about your essay-writing?

Do It Yourself

Steps

- **Step 1** Choose a topic. Based on your topic, write a thesis statement (an argument in one to two sentences) which explains the point you want to prove. You may need to do some research on your topic before you are ready to develop your thesis (see How To Develop and Implement a Research Plan, pages 85-88). The thesis should be straightforward, realistic, specific, and workable. For example, if your topic is about etiquette in the workplace, but you must cover the topic in only five paragraphs, you may need to narrow your focus to one area of workplace etiquette, such as phone etiquette.

- **Step 2** Focus on your thesis, listing the major points' and examples that can prove it. If you are writing about a piece of literature, don't retell the plot. Instead use plot features to support your thesis. Research your topic if necessary (see How to Develop and Implement a Research Plan, pages 85-88).

- **Step 3** Choose a specific title that relates to your thesis.

- **Step 4** Think about what your points mean and how they relate to each other. Make an outline of your essay. The outline will provide the skeleton for your essay. It should illustrate your thesis point by point. It is a good idea to use one major point for each paragraph.

- **Step 5** The body of your essay could use any one, or a combination, of any of the following organizational patterns:
  - cause and effect (explain that because this happened, then this will happen)
  - problem-solution (argue that this is the problem and this is the proposed solution)
  - classification (categorize your ideas or issues)
  - positives and negatives (refer to the good points and then the bad points)

- similarities and differences (explain what your points have in common and then how they are different)
- chronological (develop your points in the order things happen)
- proof by reasons or examples (give all of the reasons and specific proof)

The points you list in your outline should help you decide on the best organizational pattern for the body paragraphs.

Write your essay draft following the format in the model (page 98). Use the active voice ("This shows…" instead of "It may be shown that…"). If you are writing a familiar essay, your tone is informal and chatty (uses the word "I," contractions, some slang terms). If you are writing a formal essay, your tone is usually serious and your word choice is proper (no slang terms, fewer contractions, little use of the word "I"). In your conclusion, summarize your argument.

Step 6 Revise your essay (see How to Revise a Draft, pages 89-94). Try to vary your sentence structure and your punctuation. Make sure your essay is appropriate for your audience. Your word choice should be clear and specific. Avoid clichés, for example, "out of the frying pan and into the fire." Make sure you have used an active voice and that you have used your tense consistently. (Usually essays are written in the present tense.) Add any connecting words or phrases. Have a peer read and critique your work.

Step 7 Type or neatly write your essay, single-sided. Leave one-inch margins at the top, the bottom and on the sides of the page. Number your pages consecutively in the upper right corner. (Never number page one.) If your essay is a research essay, see How to Cite Sources, pages 100-105, to learn how to use parenthetical references and cite sources.

Hot tips
- Leave some time between writing your outline and writing your draft. Read your outline again to see if your feelings on the topic have changed. Change your outline if necessary.
- Remember to use words and phrases to link ideas and paragraphs in your essay.

Is the language in the following essay formal or informal?

> Model

What I Have Lived For
by Bertrand Russell

Three passions, simple but overwhelmingly strong, have governed my life: the longing for love, the search for knowledge, and unbearable pity for the suffering of mankind. These passions, like great winds, have blown me hither and thither, on a wayward course, over a deep ocean of anguish, reaching to the very verge of despair. *(introductory paragraph)*

I have sought love, first, because it brings ecstasy—ecstasy so sweet that I would often have sacrificed all the rest of life for a few hours of this joy. I have sought it, next, because it relieves loneliness—that terrible loneliness in which one shivering consciousness looks over the rim of the world into the cold unfathomable lifeless abyss. I have sought it, finally, because in the union of love I have seen, in a mystic miniature, the prefiguring vision of the heaven that saints and poets have imagined. This is what I sought, and though it might seem too good for human life, this is what—at last—I have found. *(first body paragraph; introductory sentence, supporting sentences, concluding sentence)*

With equal passion I have sought knowledge. I have wished to understand the hearts of men. I have wished to know why the stars shine. And I have tried to apprehend the Pythagorean power by which number holds sway above the flux. A little of this, but not much, I have achieved. *(second body paragraph)*

Love and knowledge, so far as they were possible, led upward toward the heavens. But always pity brought me back to earth. Echoes of cries of pain reverberate in my heart. Children in famine, victims tortured by oppressors, helpless old people a hated burden to their sons, and the whole world of loneliness, poverty, and pain makes a mockery of what human life should be. I long to alleviate the evil, but I cannot, and I too suffer. *(third body paragraph)*

This has been my life. I have found it worth living, and would gladly live it again if the chance were offered me. *(concluding paragraph)*

Think about It

The essay in the model is a traditional five-paragraph essay. What are the advantages and disadvantages of this essay format?

Use the Anthology

Read "Adversity" (pages 13-15). State the author's thesis and list some of the points he uses to prove his thesis.

Activities

1. Write an essay explaining your point of view on a workplace issue.
2. Write a formal research essay about a course theme (see How to Develop and Implement a Research Plan, pages 85-88.).

How to Cite Sources

Before You Start

Writers get ideas and information from a variety of sources, such as the Internet, textbooks, magazines, and films. It is the writer's job to cite where he or she found the ideas or information. Using another person's work without citing it is not acceptable; it is known as plagiarism.

To be safe, accurate, and ethical, quote and acknowledge work that is not your own. If your school has a policy on academic honesty, review it and follow it. By acknowledging the sources of your information, you are giving its authors due credit and informing your reader about your research.

Before you follow the steps for citing sources, think about the following questions:

- Have you ever seen citations in writing before? What did they look like?
- Have you recently cited sources? Did you make sure to cite all the sources that you used?
- Why do you think it is unethical to use information without citing it?

Do It Yourself

Steps

Step 1 Record the complete bibliographic information of all of your sources as you gather your information (author's name, title, editor's name, edition, number of volumes, name of series, city of publication, date of publication, page number, and Web site address).

Step 2 As you gather your information, decide what you need to paraphrase and what you would like to quote. When you put the information in your own words, you are paraphrasing. You don't need to use quotation marks, but you do have to acknowledge where you got the information.

If you choose to quote the author, copy the quotation word for word from the source. Use the same punctuation and capitalization that the author did. Record the page numbers with your notes. Here's a simple rule for deciding what to cite: you don't need to cite material that appears in three or more sources (for example, if you look up the name of Canada's prime minister in 1985, you don't need to acknowledge your source because this information is commonly available).

- **Step 3** Work the quotations carefully into your writing. Try to quote only what is necessary and relates to your argument. Introduce quotations with your own words and the correct punctuation. When you use quotation marks, your sentence must still make sense. If you need to make any changes to the quoted material, such as verb tense, use square brackets ([ ]) around your adjustments. If you choose to leave out some words in your quotations, use an ellipsis (…).

- **Step 4** Format your quotations properly.

    Include **short quotations** as part of the text of your writing. Use quotation marks, and double-space the lines like the rest of your text.

    For **quotations that are longer** than four typed lines, indent five spaces on each side of the quote and double-space. You don't need to use quotation marks because the indentation shows that you are quoting. Introduce the quotation by using a full sentence followed by a colon.

    If you need to quote **fewer than four lines of poetry**, include them as part of your text. Use quotation marks, and use a slash (/) to show where each line ends.

- **Step 5** A reference in parentheses, or brackets, is called a parenthetical reference. Use it in the body of your writing to refer to quoted or paraphrased material. Give the author's last name and the page where you found the information. The reference should immediately follow the last sentence of the material you quoted or paraphrased, before a period (for example, "…and it ended" (Suzuki, 109).) Include the complete publication information in the Works Cited section of your work.

    If the work you are citing doesn't have an author, give the title instead. If you have cited more than one work by the same author, give the title as well. If there are several authors, list all of their last names. If you are citing a play, you can give the act, scene, and line, instead of the page number (I, ii, 5-9).

- **Step 6** Explain the significance of each quotation. Let your reader know why you thought it was important to include. For instance, if you are giving a statistic on work injuries for a report, tell what you think the statistic indicates.

- **Step 7** Create a list of cited works that notes the research materials you used. You will include this list at the end of your piece of writing on a new, numbered page. Type the title Works Cited and centre it 2.5 cm from the top of the page. Double-space everything. Begin each entry at the left margin. If the entry is longer than one line, indent the following lines five spaces from the margin. Alphabetize the entries by the author's last name. If the author's name is not given, use the first major word in the title.

HOT tips

- Use index cards to organize your research. Record each source on a separate card as you research. Organize your cards in alphabetical order, then write your list of sources.
- Ignore *A, An,* and *The* in the titles of sources of sources when you alphabetize.
- Create a Works Consulted page to list sources you read but didn't quote in your work.
- Different style guides, such as *The Chicago Manual of Style*, prefer different ways of citing sources. Choose one guide, either that you like or that your teacher or librarian recommends, and use its style consistently to cite sources.
- In older works, you might find footnotes, endnotes, and a bibliography. The first two are the same as parenthetical references, but are found at the bottom of the page or the end of the book. A bibliography lists print sources; Works Cited is a more accurate title for the listing of research resources now that non-print sources, such as the Internet, are used for research as well.

How to Cite Sources **103**

Here are some examples of sources cited. Use these models as a guide to citing sources.

Model 1

Parenthetical References

Dave believes that by consulting the barber he "had taken the first step along the road to financial prosperity" (Chilton, 30).

if *The Wealthy Barber* is the only book by the author in your Works Cited, just give the page number of the quotation (30)

if you have another work by David Chilton, include the title in the reference (Chilton, *The Wealthy Barber*, 30)

Model 2

Works Cited

Chilton, David. *The Wealthy Barber: The Common Sense Guide to Successful Financial Planning.* Toronto: Stoddart, 1989.

author's last name is first, followed by a comma and the first name, followed by a period

write the complete title of the book in italics

if there is more than one date of publication listed, include only the most recent

if there is more than one city listed, include only the city that is closest to you

104 Making It Work: Writing

Model 3

Works Cited

an article from a reference book begins with the title (in quotation marks) of the subject, or what you looked up

"Atwood, Margaret." *The Concise Oxford Companion to English Literature.* Ed. Margaret Drabble and Jenny Stringer. New York: Oxford UP, 1987.

how to cite two books listed by the same author

Austen, Jane. *Emma.* Ed. R. W. Chapman. 3rd ed. London: Oxford UP, 1974. Vol. 4 of *The Novels of Jane Austen.*

how to cite a multi-volume work

—. *Mansfield Park.* Ed. R. W. Chapman. 3rd ed. London: Oxford UP, 1974. Vol. 3 of *The Novels of Jane Austen.*

write CD ROM after the underlined title if the source is a CD-ROM

a government publication begins with the level of government, then the government agency

Government of Ontario, Ministry of Education. *Media Literacy: Intermediate and Senior Divisions,* 1989.

for a television episode or radio program, put the title in quotation marks first, followed by the names of the hosts and the title of the series

"The Hero's Adventure." Joseph Campbell and Bill Moyers. *The Power of Myth.* Writ. and Narr. Bill Moyers. PBS, 1986.

Herstein, H.H., J.J. Hughes, and R.C. Kirbyson. *Challenge and Survival: The History of Canada.* Scarborough: Prentice, 1970.

this textbook has more than one author

include the date and page number of the article

Holme, Betty. "Miracle Baby." *London Free Press,* 6 Jan. 1963, late ed., A14.

for a newspaper or magazine article, list the reporter's name followed by the title of the article in quotation marks

The K-W Fly-fishers. *Fly-Fishing for Fun.* Kitchener-Waterloo, 2001.

how to cite a pamphlet or a corporate publication

Long, Rose. Telephone interview. 13 Oct. 2001.

for a personal interview, list the interviewee's name first

for films, filmstrips, and slides, begin with the title

A Room with a View. Dir. James Ivory. Prod. Ismail Merchant. With Maggie Smith, Denholm Elliott, and Julian Sands. Merchant Ivory Productions, 1986. 117 min. Based on E.M. Forster's *A Room with a View.*

Smith, Jack. "Preparing for the World of Work." *Professions Today.* Ed. Tina Lee. New York: Columbia UP, 2001. 25-38.

an article from a magazine or anthology has the article title in quotation marks with the page numbers of the article at the end of the citation

"True Health and Safety Stories." Young Worker Awareness Program. Workplace Safety and Insurance Board, 2001. www.yworker.com/english/index.html. November 4, 2003.

for a Web site citation include the complete URL and the date you visited the site

Think about It

Why is it a good idea to use a variety of sources in your research?

Use the Anthology

Read the report "Analyzing the "Tween" Market" (pages 80-97). Visit the Web site (www.mediawatch.ca) to see the whole report. Find the sources used to complete the report. Describe to a partner the steps you would take to check the sources.

Activities

1. Go to the library and find at least three examples of cited sources or bibliographies on a career choice or a topic you are studying. Compare their styles. Do you prefer one style over another? Why?

2. Write a research report on your career choice or on a topic such as safety or ethics in the workplace, pay equity, or hiring practices. Try to find information from a variety of sources, such as a Web site, magazine, book, and newspaper. Create a list of cited works for the information you found. Use parenthetical references in the body of the report.

How to Prepare a Portfolio

Before You Start

A portfolio contains examples of your best work that are relevant to the purpose of your portfolio. It can help a teacher evaluate your course work or an employer discover your abilities. You can use it in a job interview to illustrate your accomplishments.

You might include some or all of these in a portfolio:

- a title page with a statement about your career goals or job objective
- a table of contents
- a list of your skills, traits, and experiences with brief explanations of how they are shown in your portfolio
- samples of your best work (for example, essays, reports, research projects, letters, brochures, videos, co-op evaluations, memos, and action plans)
- letters of recommendation as well as thank-you notes for work you did (for example, from a teacher, past employer, mentor, and/or co-op coordinator)
- a list of certificates, awards, badges, honours (for example, employee of the month award, typing proficiency certificate, attendance award, volunteer certificate)
- a list of volunteer activities you participated in and workshops, seminars, and courses you attended (for example, fund-raising walk for multiple sclerosis, first-aid course, race relations workshop, WHMIS)
- school transcripts
- references (full names, titles, relationships to you, addresses, and phone numbers)

Before you follow the steps to preparing a portfolio, think about the following questions:

- What items can you think of that would help illustrate your skills and achievements?
- Why is a portfolio a useful tool when you are searching for a job?

Do It Yourself

Steps

- **Step 1** Write, collect, update, and copy the items you want to include in your portfolio, using the list on page 106 as a guide. Include between eight and 12 items in your portfolio. Each item should show a specific skill, including some of the skills you include in your résumé. Create a table of contents for your portfolio.
- **Step 2** Decide on the format for your portfolio, such as a scrapbook, binder with dividers, accordion file, duotang, Web site, disk, or video.
- **Step 3** Ensure that your portfolio is professional, neat, organized, correct, and thorough.
- **Step 4** Look at the items you have chosen. Make sure you've kept in mind your audience (potential employer or teacher) and purpose (to get a job or do well in a course). Check that your work is sufficient and relevant.
- **Step 5** Have a peer or mentor check your work for organization, neatness, appropriateness, and focus.

HOT tips

- Keep your portfolio updated.
- Take your job portfolio with you to all interviews.
- Include a variety of work samples.

Model

title page indicates who created portfolio

Alexander Fausto
September 5, 2003
Job Portfolio

table of contents and list of skills are organizational tools

Table of Contents

1. List of skills, traits, and experience .... page 3
2. Samples of best work .... page 4
3. Letters of recommendation and thanks ..... page 10
4. List of certificates, awards, badges, and honours .... page 14
5. List of volunteer activities and work experiences .... page 15
6. School transcripts .... page 16
7. References .... page 18

the materials follow in the order listed in table of contents

How to Prepare a Portfolio | 109

List of Skills and Traits	Experiences That Demonstrate an Application of My Skills
1. Work to high standards	English essay, excellent attendance record, French presentation, letters of appreciation, history report
2. Create and follow action plans	Action plan to improve math mark, action plan to organize the school's niner night, action plan for independent study
3. Use appropriate technology	Letter of recommendation from computer teacher, including graphics software sample school newspaper layout; award for speed in keyboarding
4. Meet deadlines and manage time	Transcripts; letters of recommendation from the student council and newspaper advisors, the Pinehurst Nursing Home Supervisor, and the newspaper delivery supervisor

each skill starts with a verb for consistency

sample shows the student's skills

Alexander has had two jobs to date, but he includes other experiences to highlight his skills

Letter of Recommendation

August 5, 2003

Louisa Bax
Delivery Manager, The Local News
1243 Main Street
Elk Lake, Ontario
N2R 2P9

To Whom It May Concern:
Alexander Fausto worked as a newspaper carrier for three years. He regularly showed up for his route, collated four to seven sections of the newspaper, and served 100 homes daily. He was given considerable responsibility, collecting payments from 30 families. He kept neat and accurate records, was polite, and dependable. He has the standards and the ability to become a valuable professional.

Sincerely,

Louisa Bax

Louisa Bax

Think about It

Are the table of contents and list of skills in the model effective? Why?

Use the Anthology

Choose a character from one of the selections in *Moving On*. Write a list of the skills that that character might include in a job portfolio. Share your list with a partner, and explain why you chose each skill.

Activities

1. Create a portfolio using the steps outlined on page 107.
2. Practise a job interview with a peer, teacher, mentor, or parent as the interviewer. Use your portfolio to illustrate your skills and accomplishments. Explain why you chose each piece and what it reveals about your skills.

How to Write Instructions

Before You Start

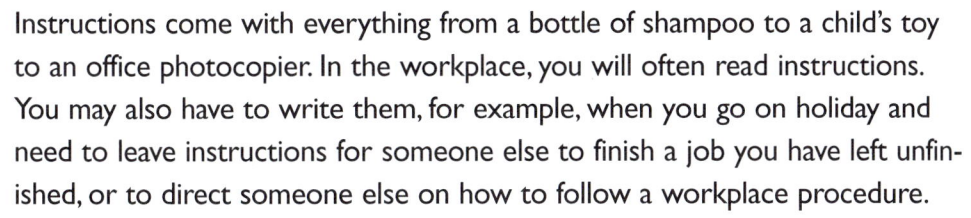

Instructions come with everything from a bottle of shampoo to a child's toy to an office photocopier. In the workplace, you will often read instructions. You may also have to write them, for example, when you go on holiday and need to leave instructions for someone else to finish a job you have left unfinished, or to direct someone else on how to follow a workplace procedure.

Before you follow the steps to writing instructions, think about these questions:
- What kinds of instructions are you used to reading?
- What makes them easy to read and follow?
- What makes them difficult to read and follow?

Do It Yourself

Steps

- **Step 1** Choose a topic about which you can write instructions, or use a topic assigned by your teacher.
- **Step 2** Decide on the purpose of your instructions. Then state the goal of the procedure, for instance, how to change the toner in the photocopier. Remember your purpose and audience as you write.
- **Step 3** List everything that the reader needs to prepare in order to complete the activity. You might call this section Preparation, Getting Started, or Read Me First.
- **Step 4** Give this next section a title, such as Instructions, Steps, or Procedure. List all of the steps needed to do the activity. Write them in the imperative mood, beginning with an active verb, if possible. Use active voice ("Remove the toner cartridge."). Use parallel structure for your instructions, such as a list with each item beginning with a verb. It would be a good idea to use second person consistently, with the "you" understood, as in the model above.

- **Step 5** Arrange the steps in proper order.
- **Step 6** Consider adding tips after the steps if you have any advice for your audience.
- **Step 7** Follow the steps you have written to make sure you have not forgotten anything important.
- **Step 8** Revise your instructions so that they are clear, simple, and concise. Include a title. Check your grammar and spelling. Make sure your punctuation and capitalization are consistent.
- **Step 9** Format your instructions. Experiment with boxes, subheads, and graphics. Use hyphens or points for unordered lists and numbers for ordered lists. When you choose your font type and size, pick something easy to read and attractive. Use type formats (bold, italics, shading) sparingly and consistently. Balance your use of white space. For a longer set of instructions, or an instruction manual, you could include a title page, table of contents, and appendix.

HOT tips
- Some manuals include a section on potential problems and how to fix them.
- Read various manuals, including this one, for more examples of formatting.

Here are some written instructions. What do you like about how they are written?

Model 1

How to Have a Successful First Day of Work

Getting Ready
Find out what you can about the company, its location, your hours, whom you report to, and the dress code.

Instructions

steps are in chronological order

1. Dress appropriately.
2. Bring lunch and/or money.
3. Show up on time and at the right place.
4. Smile and try to relax.
5. Pay attention and ask questions.
6. Take notes about the tasks you will have to preform.
7. Be aware of what is safe and appropriate. Speak up if a task seems dangerous or makes you uncomfortable.
8. Be friendly to your new co-workers but save long conversations for breaks.
9. Return from breaks on time.
10. Make sure you understand your responsibilities and know what you have to do the next day.
11. Leave a tidy work space.

steps are in the imperative mood, beginning with verbs, and in active voice (they sound like commands)

Tips

You can ask for policies and procedures from the Human Resources Department.

You should now be ready to make a great first impression and start a successful career.

Think about It

Is there anything you would add to this model? If so, what?

Use the Anthology

Read "Finding and Keeping a Sense of Accomplishment and Worth" (pages 68-69). Turn Jonathon's exercise into a set of instructions for others to follow.

Activities

1. Find an instruction manual at home or in the school office. Examine its format and content. Write an assessment of the manual, commenting on the tone, usability, organization, and layout of the manual. Include at least one suggestion for improving the manual and explain your choice.

2. Write instructions for an activity of your choice. Here are some possible topics: first-aid, job safety, etiquette on the job, starting a business, applying for a job.

How to Write a Report for the Workplace

Before You Start

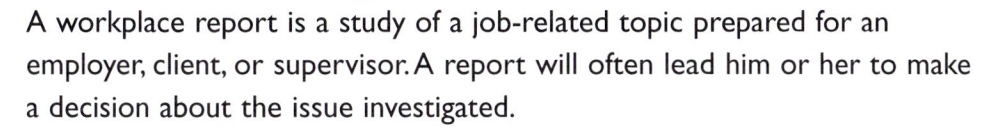

A workplace report is a study of a job-related topic prepared for an employer, client, or supervisor. A report will often lead him or her to make a decision about the issue investigated.

A report usually includes these elements:

- title page
- abstract (one-paragraph summary of the report)
- table of contents
- introduction
- a statement of purpose
- an explanation of why the report needs to be made
- a description of methods used to create the report (for example, Internet search on makes and models, calls to the manufacturers about recalls, manufacturer brochures and manuals, thorough examination of the equipment)
- the body of the report, giving the findings of the study (with interpretations and suggestions, if appropriate), including graphs, charts, lists, maps
- conclusion, summarizing the significance of the research and possibly including a recommendation
- appendix (information you want to include that doesn't fit into the body)
- list of works cited

Before you follow the steps to writing a report for the workplace, think about the following questions:

- What reports have you written?
- How is a report similar to an essay? How is it different?
- Why do you think reports are an important way to communicate in the workplace?

Do It Yourself

Steps

- **Step 1** — Choose a topic. Consider a problem, need, or question related to a specific workplace.

- **Step 2** — Decide on the purpose of your report. Ask yourself what your audience needs to know and how readers will use your report. Remember your purpose and audience as you write.

- **Step 3** — Figure out the key points that are your focus. Consider starting with Who? What? Where? When? Why? and How? Decide what information you need and how you will gather it.

- **Step 4** — Research your topic. Conduct interviews to add authority to your report. Document all of your sources (see How to Cite Sources, pages 100-105).

- **Step 5** — Draft your report. You can use paragraphs, lists, graphs, and charts — whatever works best for organizing your ideas.

- **Step 6** — Write in a plain, concise style and a formal tone. Use the second person (you) or third person (he/she) point of view consistently.

- **Step 7** — Check the content of your report. Did you accomplish your purpose? Have you given your readers what they need? Is the abstract faithful to the report? Does the introduction give a statement of purpose, an explanation of why the report is needed, and a description of how the findings were done? Is the body logically developed? Does the conclusion summarize the findings and make a recommendation?

- **Step 8** — Revise your report so it is clear. Check your grammar and spelling. Make sure your punctuation and capitalization are consistent. Have a peer check your work.

- **Step 9** — Format your report. Use design elements to make it easy for your readers to find what they need. Experiment with headings, subheadings, and graphics. Use bold, italics, and/or shading sparingly and consistently. The white space should be balanced.

HOT tips
- If you have written a book report, use that experience to help you draft your workplace report.
- If you don't have a job, ask someone who does about an important issue in his or her workplace.

Here is part of a workplace report. What sections of it are included? What information do you think you will get from each section?

Model

Investigation of the Daisy Daycare's Playground Equipment

by Ming Nguyen

August 10, 2002

— title page

Abstract

The Daisy Daycare has been operating for 10 years at 12 Seaview Lane. In accordance with county regulations, the owners have undertaken a safety check of the daycare's outdoor playground equipment to ensure that all standards are being met. This report will look at the safety standards, assess the current equipment, and make a recommendation about keeping or replacing the equipment.

— introduction
— issue to be addressed
— what the report will show

Table of Contents

table of contents

table of contents and abstract wouldn't be needed in short report

Abstract 2

Introduction 3

Body 4

Conclusion 9

Appendix 10

Works Cited 11

Introduction

Purpose

first sentence – purpose

second sentence – aim

third sentence – longer description of methods used to create the report

This report investigates the safety of the Daisy Daycare's playground equipment. Before a child is injured, it is necessary to find out when and where the outdoor equipment was made and whether or not it is still safe. This analysis of the outdoor equipment involves an Internet search on the makes and models, calls to the manufacturers about recalls and complaints, an analysis of manufacturer brochures and manuals, and a thorough examination of the equipment.

Think about It

A police officer's incident report, a salesperson's sales report, and a biologist's environmental study all use the same basic report-writing format, outlined on page 116. What are the advantages of this format?

Use the Anthology

Read "The Grand River Conservation Authority 2000 Annual Report" (pages 183-188). How does it compare to the model on pages 117-118 of this handbook? Why do you think there are differences?

Activities

1. Find a workplace report to examine. Check the library, the Internet, your school, a local community centre, or another public forum whose reports are available for reading. Evaluate the form and content of the report, answering the following questions and explaining your responses: How is the report organized? Is the organization effective? Does the report do what it says it will do in the introduction and abstract? Are the findings conveyed clearly? How do graphs, maps, figures, or charts add to the report? Is the conclusion sound?

2. Write a workplace report. Consider using a workplace you are familiar with from a summer job, co-op placement, or workplace visit.

How to Write a Poem

Before You Start

Writing poetry allows you to play with words and express yourself. It is a way to understand yourself, others, and the world in general. Experimenting with poetry can help you become comfortable writing about your feelings, and help you use more images and concrete details when writing in others formats or styles.

There is no one formula for writing a poem. However, using the steps below can help you think about a topic, organize your thoughts, and use language in different ways to share your ideas.

Before you follow the steps to share your ideas through poetry, think about these questions:
- What is the difference between prose and poetry? How would you define poetry?
- What poems have you read that you have enjoyed? What have you liked about them?

Do It Yourself

Steps

- **Step 1** Think of possible topics that have meaning for you. Poems have been written about every topic imaginable. You may want to write an idea bank of words, images, phrases, and experiences. You can also get inspiration from an outside source. For example, find a piece of art, a film, a photograph, or music that you think is interesting. List what you notice about it — sounds, instruments, colours, lines, textures, missing objects, missing words, and so on.

- **Step 2** Find a place where you can think and relax. Look at any words you have written, or again look at or listen to your outside source carefully.

- **Step 3** Write your thoughts on paper. Your poem can rhyme or be free verse (a poem that doesn't rhyme).

  Here are some suggestions for getting started:

  – Poems often appeal to the senses. Brainstorm some sensory images, similes, and metaphors. (See Line Master 2, available from your teacher, for more information on these devices).

- Think of a mood you would like to convey, an interesting situation you were in, a fascinating place you visited or thing you saw, a dream you had, a significant memory, or a unique person you met.
- Brainstorm some images you would like to include in your poem, then cluster them as they connect to each other.
- Look through your journals and turn your favourite passages into a poem.
- If you are using an outside source, list all the things in or about it that might be able to speak — the artist, a person in the artwork or song, the subject of the artwork or song. What might he/she/it say if it could? When you have a strong sense of this, begin to write your poem. Keep returning to the source for ideas.

Write your poem without revising it as you go along. You can do that after the poem is finished.

- **Step 4** Think about your draft poem. Consider these questions to help you experiment with your poem:

  - What makes your writing a poem?
  - Does your poem convey what you wanted it to convey?
  - Have you used colourful images?
  - Does your poem give a strong sense of your ideas about an artwork or song?
  - What is the theme or main idea of your poem? Is it clear?
  - What is the mood or feeling in your poem? Is it effective?
  - Are there any sounds or rhymes you want to add to your poem?
  - Did you use any symbols or allusions? Do you want to add any?
  - Did you use a pattern? If so, do you like the pattern, or can you rework the poem into a pattern that fits the poem better?
  - If you used rhyme, consider whether any of your lines is awkward or forced. You can use a rhyming dictionary to help you rework some of the rhymes.

- **Step 5** Revise your poem until you are happy with it. Re-examine your word choice. Take out unnecessary words, or any words that you think don't fit. You have poetic license, a freedom to break the rules of punctuation, language, and spelling so you can spell the words how they sound, or use no punctuation at all if you want. Read the poem aloud and have peers read it aloud to hear how it sounds.
- **Step 6** Arrange the words of your poem on the page so the lines end where you want them to end. The pause at the end of the line is half as long as you would pause for a comma. If you want, you can make your poem into a shape on the page.
- **Step 7** Type or write your good copy. Include an appropriate title.

Hot tips

- Use poetic devices (such as similes, metaphors, personification) only a few times, or you may distract your audience.
- Work on a few poems at once so that you aren't too frustrated if you don't like one of them.

This free-verse poem was written through stream of consciousness (recording thoughts that come into one's head at random). What do you think of the topic?

Model

Road Kill

by Claire Kerr

There was once this guy who ran over a dog and the dog got killed, so he knocked on this one door and this one lady who owned the dog told him that he could go to hell and that her dog cost 50 bucks, so there.

That dog wasn't a dog though, no he wasn't a dog even though that one lady bought him for 50 bucks.

The dog was another creature, one that pretended to be a dog, a dead dog hit by the guy in the car, but he wasn't a dog, the one lady thought he was, but the dog that wasn't one knew what he was.

He was a parrot.

A parrot in a dog's body.

The parrot liked being a dog even the bits with check-ups and doghouses.

The parrot enjoyed bones and cars and cats and that one lady who called him Chucky and let him sleep on the sofa and bought him for 50 bucks after he stopped being a parrot and started being a dog, one that got run over.

The dog that used to be a parrot thought that living in the City and eating meat was better than parroting in Africa, the place he had been before, and dying before he was three.

The dog that stopped being a parrot didn't mind getting run over by that one guy because he had stopped being a dog, and good thing that one lady didn't know too.

He had started being aquatic.

He had started being a fish.

He had started being a fish, a big one, with normal gills and pretty scales.

And it was all kind of funny, cos he got bought by this other lady for 5 bucks at Kensington the day after that.

Think about It

What elements of this poem are also found in stories? What elements make it a poem?

Use the Anthology

Read the poems "Me as My Grandmother" (page 4) and "The Stickhandler" (pages 148-149). As a class, discuss what you think the inspiration was for each poem. Then decide which topic inspires you personally, and write a poem about that topic.

Activities

1. **a.** Start collecting poems you can find around you, such as those in greeting cards, commercials, billboards, Web sites, music videos, and songs. Where do you find poems in the newspaper? What poems are at school? What poems are in the workplace?
   b. Discuss in a small group how this activity has expanded your idea of what a poem is.
2. Gather a number of poems to read aloud. Think about the best way to say or perform the poems, and then present your favourites to the class.

Language

TABLE OF CONTENTS

Using Your Language Competently and Confidently	126
How to Expand Your Vocabulary	129
How to Give Oral Instructions Effectively	134
How to Become an Effective Listener	138
How to Create an Effective Speaking Style	143
How to Create and Give Effective Oral Presentations	148
How to Communicate in a Group	156
How to Create Your Own Voice in Writing	162

Using Your Language Competently and Confidently

One of the first impressions you make on others is through the way you use language. Who you are speaking to and interacting with will influence your choice of words and tone of voice. You'll speak differently with your co-workers from the way you would with your employer, just as you speak differently with your friends from the way you would with your parents or a community leader. You may be speaking English with everyone, but you use different levels of English each time. When you know which of your levels of English to use, you'll make the right impression on your audience.

▶ Levels of language

Generally, we use three levels of language with our different audiences: formal language, informal language, and colloquial language, or slang. Here are some examples of the three levels of language:

Formal	Informal	Slang
abundance	plenty of	heaps, lots, loads
father	daddy, dad	pop, pa
banquet	meal	grub, eats, a feed
oration	speech, talk	spiel, hot air, gab, bull

Create three columns on a page. Label one column as "Formal Language," one as "Informal Language," and one as "Slang." Then examine each of the following words. (Use a dictionary if you need to find the meanings of any of the words.) Place each one in its proper column.

demise	stuck up	guy
swipe	slumber	simpleton
duds	residence	inebriated
frugal	cop	demented
eccentric	lazy	scram
skinny	scam	automobile
mad	hobo	weary

▸ How levels of language affect meaning

Try this exercise. It will help you to see how your choice of levels of language can affect meaning when you write or speak.

- Read the words in your "Formal Language" column. Write a brief paragraph that tells a story suggested by the words in the list. Make sure your paragraph includes each word in the list.
- Now examine the words in your "Slang" list. Write a different paragraph using all of the words in the column.
- Finally, repeat the exercise with the words in your "Informal Language" list.

Read the three paragraphs to yourself or to a partner. How do the words in each paragraph affect its meaning? What impression of the writer do you get from each paragraph? How are these impressions different?

Knowing how and when to use each level of language appropriately is a key skill. This unit will give you opportunities to expand your vocabulary, and to use each level of language in appropriate situations. You will also learn other important language skills, including how to work effectively in a group, how to be a good listener, how to give oral instructions, and how to become an effective speaker.

How to Expand Your Vocabulary

Before You Start

Most of us are comfortable with the words that we use from our personal vocabularies when we speak and write. But developing a larger vocabulary can help make your speaking and writing more interesting, and can help you make a good impression in a résumé or letter of application. In the workplace, people expand their vocabulary with the specialized terminology that is part of their job. Expand your vocabulary now by keeping a personal dictionary to record words and terms that you read and hear; by using a thesaurus to choose new and interesting words for your writing; and by using a dictionary to check word meanings.

Before you follow the steps to expand your vocabulary, think about these questions:

- What do you do when you have trouble understanding a word?
- What do you do when you want to make your writing more interesting?
- What strategies would you use to help you learn new vocabulary for a new job?

Do It Yourself

Step 1 Reread a recent piece of writing you have created.
- Underline the words you've overused.
- Highlight words you've used that you think could be more interesting and effective.
- Circle any words you've used whose meanings you're unsure of.

- **Step 2** Use a thesaurus to find more interesting or effective words to replace each of the words you've highlighted and underlined.

  > A thesaurus is a reference book that lists synonyms for words. Using a thesaurus is a good way to expand your vocabulary. To use a thesaurus, do the following:
  > - Look up the word.
  > - Read the synonyms.
  > - Read how the synonyms are used, then decide which synonym will best fit your writing.
  > - Replace the overused or less-effective word with the one you've selected from the thesaurus.
  > - Reread the sentence with its new word. Think about whether the new word will help a reader understand your writing.
  > - If the word doesn't seem to fit in the sentence or match your own meaning, go back to the thesaurus and choose another word.

- **Step 3** Look at the words you've circled. Look in the dictionary to check their meaning. A dictionary can tell you many things about a word, including:

  > - how the word is divided into syllables
  > - how the word is pronounced
  > - the word's function in a sentence (part of speech)
  > - different forms of the word (plurals, verb tenses, noun forms)
  > - the history of the word (what language it comes from)
  > - the definition of the word
  > - how the word can be used in a sentence
  > - special meanings of the word
  > - synonyms (words with similar meanings) and antonyms (opposites) for the word

  Read the entry to learn as much as you can about the word. If you have misspelled or misused a word, change it.

- **Step 4** You can also learn new words and their meanings without looking them up in the dictionary. You can find the meaning from the context, or the words surrounding the word. Meanings of words are often given in the sentence itself in the following ways:

   - By definition: He circumnavigated, or sailed around, the world.
   - By examples: Travel is simplified by the use of conveyances such as cars, bicycles, airplanes, and boats.
   - By synonyms: Peter's narcissistic tendencies only prove he is conceited.
   - By contrast: Mei is svelte, unlike Alejandro, who is heavy.
   - By cause and effect: The precipice was steep, so we backed away from its edge.

- **Step 5** Keep a personal dictionary, or a list of words and their meanings that you find in your reading, conversations, and viewing. Use these new and interesting words in your writing.

HOT tips

- The biggest words aren't always the best words to use. Make sure that the words you use match your purpose and your audience.
- Keep your personal dictionary beside you when you're reading or viewing. Write down any interesting words you find. After you've finished reading or watching, look up the word's meaning in the dictionary and note it.
- If you've replaced one word with another, always reread the sentence to yourself. If the word doesn't fit or sound right, find another one.

Making It Work: Language

Model 1 and Model 2 are samples of a dictionary entry and a thesaurus entry. Which one is which? How do you know?

Model 1

aw.ful (of'el) *adj.*1. Extremely bad or unpleasant; terrible. 2. Commanding or inspiring awe. 3. Filled with awe, esp. filled with or displaying great reverence. 4. Formidable in nature or extent. –*adv. Informal.* Extremely; very. [ME *aweful,* awe-inspiring, blend of *awe,* awe; see AWE and *ayfull, awful (<OE *egefull: ege,* dread + *full,* -ful.] –**aw'ful.ly** *adv.* –aw'ful.ness *n.*

Model 2

Awful- adj. Appalling, ugly, dreadful, solemn, horrendous, deplorable, ghastly, hideous, portentous. (unalarming, alluring, terrific, pretty, unnoticeable, likeable, delightful, unimposing).

Think about It

Write a sentence using the word "awful." Then write two more versions of your sentence, each time using a different synonym for "awful" from Model 2. Which of the three versions of your sentence do you think is most effective? Why?

Use the Anthology

Choose a selection from *Moving On* that you have already read and re-read it. List any words whose meaning you do not know. Use one of the methods described in Steps 2 to 5 on pages 130-131 to help you understand the words.

Activities

1. **a.** Using a dictionary, learn all you can about the words listed below. Then use each one in a sentence.

genial	benevolence	leniency	condor	benefactor
humane	arrogant	malicious	pilgrimage	avarice
encounter	vagabond	provocative		

   b. Which of these words might you use in your own writing? Why?

2. Add words to your personal dictionary from:
   - a magazine article you've read
   - lyrics to a song you like or one that presents an interesting point of view
   - descriptions in a magazine or television ad
   - a film or video you've viewed

3. Select six or seven interesting words from your personal dictionary that seem to go together either in meaning or in sound. Create a poem from the words.

How to Give Oral Instructions Effectively

Before You Start

In your life and work, you'll often be asked to give someone else instructions or directions. The ability to give good instructions will make you a valued co-worker, employee, or manager.

When you give instructions, you "instruct" a listener in completing a task that usually has many steps. Through your instructions, you help someone to know how to complete the task from beginning to end. The secret to giving good instructions is to give the steps in the right order, to keep the steps short, and to speak clearly with your eye on the listener.

Before you follow the steps to giving oral instructions, think about these questions:

- What do you listen for when someone gives you instructions?
- When would you have to give instructions in the workplace?

Do It Yourself

Steps

- **Step 1** Before you give the instructions, make sure you clearly understand them yourself. Review the steps in your mind before you address your listener.
- **Step 2** If there are many steps in the process you will be explaining, encourage your listener to make brief notes as you talk.
- **Step 3** Begin your instructions with words that signal the first step, such as "First" or "Begin by." For each new step in the instructions, use a signal word, such as "Next" or "Then." Speak clearly and slowly. Keep the steps short.

- **Step 4** Use body language and gestures to emphasize the order of the steps as you speak. You might number the steps on your fingers, "one," "two," "three," and so on as a visual cue for the listener. Use direction words like "up" and "down" to help the listener visualize what to do.

- **Step 5** Pause between steps to give the listener time to process the information. Make eye contact with the listener after each step. This will help you to see if the listener has understood.

- **Step 6** When you've completed giving the instructions, give the listener a brief summary, like this: "So this is what you do: first you _____, then _____. When that's taken care of, do _____. Finally, you do _____."

- **Step 7** Ask the listener if he or she has any questions.

- **Step 8** Ask the listener to repeat the steps back to you in their proper order. If the listener has missed a step, explain again what to do.

Hot tips

- Be clear.
- Explain each step as briefly as you can.
- Use the simplest words possible, but use technical language when it's necessary.
- Use gestures and body language to help the listener understand your instructions.
- Always look at your listener to help you see how well he or she understands.

This is a set of instructions for the series of yoga postures called a Sun Salutation. What signal words do you notice that would help someone to follow these instructions more easily?

Model

1. First, stand as tall as you can.
2. Then clasp your hands in front of you, palms touching, fingers pointing to the sky and elbows up.
3. Next, lean back from the waist, gently. Hold this stretch to the count of three.
4. Then come forward carefully and touch your toes. Place your palms on the floor if you can.
5. Now send your right leg back, and then send your left leg back until you are in push-up position.
6. Lower your knees carefully to the floor. Then lower your abdomen. Gently arch your back and hold this position.
7. Next, release the pose and push down with your hands. Raise your hips up into an inverted V position. Hold this pose to the count of three.
8. Now bring your right leg through your arms and place your foot on the floor between your hands. Do the same with your left leg.
9. Finally, return slowly to the standing position and relax.

Think about It

If you were following these instructions, what would you want the instructor to do to make sure that you could complete the Sun Salutation successfully?

Use the Anthology

Read the employment application (pages 163-164). Give a partner instructions for completing it (for example, be accurate, print your answers).

Activities

1. The lessons in this book give instructions about how to read, how to write, and how to use language and media. Turn to How to Write a Memorandum on pages 78-80.
   - Read the Do It Yourself section a number of times until you understand the order of the steps.
   - Next, tell your partner how to write a memo, step by step, using the steps in this lesson.
   - Each of you will then write a memo to someone about a school issue.
   - When you finish your memo, check the instructions again in Do It Yourself. How well did you follow the instructions?

2. Give your partner instructions for doing a Sun Salutation. Experiment with giving the instructions in two ways:
   - First, read all of the instructions aloud to a partner. Then ask the partner to do the Sun Salutation without further help from you. How successful was your partner in following the instructions?
   - Now, guide your partner through the Sun Salutation one step at a time, giving him or her a chance to complete each step before you give the instruction for the next.

   Which of these two approaches was the most successful? Why?

3. Write a set of instructions for playing a board game, fixing something, cooking something, or managing time. Give the instructions orally to a partner, and have your partner follow them. When you are done, ask your partner to tell what was easy and what was challenging about following your instructions. Repeat this activity by following instructions that your partner gives you. When you've finished, identify with your partner the three most important things to remember when you're giving instructions.

How to Become an Effective Listener

Before You Start

In life and on the job, we usually put time and effort into speaking. We also need to put time and effort into listening. When we invest time in listening, we can be more efficient and effective in our tasks and our work, and we get more satisfaction from working with others.

Good listeners make good co-workers and employees because:

— they are efficient at their work. They listen for information, follow instructions accurately, and they don't need a lot of information repeated to enable them to complete the task.
— they show that they care about people — their customers, managers, and fellow workers. They give their interest and attention to the speaker.
— they contribute to the success of their company or organization. They listen critically to what is said and interpret what is important.

How well we listen depends on three conditions:
— how we're feeling and what we're concerned about at the time
— how we feel about the person we're listening to, and the experiences we've had previously with him or her
— our purpose and reason for listening

There are three main reasons for listening to others.
— to show attention or interest in the speaker (appreciative listening)
— to listen for information (content listening)
— to analyze or interpret what the speaker is saying (critical listening)

Before you follow the steps to becoming an effective listener, think about these questions:
- How would you rate your listening skills?
- What situations have you been in that have required you to listen attentively?
- What strategies do you use to listen effectively?

Do It Yourself

Step 1 Be an **appreciative listener**. To show that you're interested in what the speaker has to say, try some of the following:
- Make eye contact with the speaker.
- Make the distance between you a comfortable one — not too close and not too far away.
- Lean toward the speaker.
- Keep your own body open. Relax your posture.
- Find out whether the speaker wants your advice or just wants to talk.
- Ask questions or make supportive statements at key points while you're listening. That will show the speaker that you're paying attention.
- Smile or show appropriate emotion as the speaker is talking.
- Don't fidget, look away, or look at your watch, unless you want to signal to the speaker that you've run out of time.

Step 2 When you're **listening** mainly to **get information** from the speaker, try the following:
- Listen for the speaker's signal words that tell you how many key points, ideas, or details to listen for. For example, "There are three basic things to remember about…" Then "check off" each item in your mind as you hear it.
- Try to visualize, or "see," the information the speaker is giving you. For example, if the speaker is giving directions, try to see yourself doing each step, or see yourself following a route.
- "Chunk" similar information and details together in your mind or on paper. For example, when you're getting information about how to arrange stock on shelves, put like things together in your mind as you're listening. Even better, draw a diagram with empty blocks. Then write the names of the different stock items in blocks to show their proper placement.
- Keep a pen and notepad in your pocket, purse, or backpack. If the speaker is giving many details quickly, write down lists of items in your notepad. You can always read these over later. Turn them into checklists and reminders for when you're doing your work.
- Always ask the speaker to repeat something that wasn't clear or that you didn't understand. If the speaker isn't available, then ask someone else who has heard the same message. Compare what you've heard to confirm the information.

- **Step 3** Be a **critical listener**. Analyze what you have heard, and interpret or evaluate the message.
  - When you interpret what you've heard, you ask yourself: "What does this really mean?" That requires you to make inferences, or to read between the lines.
  - A good place to start is to ask yourself what it means to you. Then think of someone who is very different from yourself, and ask what the message might mean to him or her. Then decide which meaning the speaker intended.
  - When people speak, a great deal of meaning is in their tone. Sometimes the speaker's meaning is the opposite of what the words say. For example, a speaker may say, "What a peaceful world we are leaving to our children!" If she says it in a sarcastic tone, you know that the speaker means just the opposite — that the world is not a peaceful place. You interpret the meaning through listening to and understanding the speaker's tone.
  - When you evaluate what you've heard, you ask yourself: "Is this true? Is it believable? Is it right?" or, "Is this fact or someone's opinion?" To evaluate a message, it's very important to be able to tell the difference between fact and opinion.
  - A **fact** is a statement that can be verified. You can find out if it is true or not from a variety of sources. To evaluate facts, you may have to do your own research to know if they are true.
  - An **opinion** is someone's interpretation of the facts. An opinion isn't necessarily true, even if the speaker believes that it is. There are many different ways to interpret facts. When you listen critically, you decide whether or not the speaker has explained the facts in a believable way. To evaluate an opinion, it is often helpful to keep an open mind and to judge the value of what was said only after you've heard the complete opinion.

How to Become an Effective Listener

> **H•T tips**
> - Prepare yourself to listen.
> - Listening isn't just waiting for your turn to talk. Listening means giving all of your attention to the person who's speaking.
> - When you're listening, listen also for the meaning you get from the speaker's tone of voice and body language. Sometimes what the speaker is not saying can be just as important as his or her words. Look for the clues.
> - Listen with an open mind. If you've already made up your mind about the topic or the speaker before the speech, you won't learn very much. You'll end up in the same place you started.
> - When the speaker has finished, give a meaningful response. The speaker is then more likely to listen to you while you're talking.

The following passage from the book *The Perfect Storm* gives facts and details about the sword-fishing boat *Andrea Gail,* which was lost at sea in a storm in the fall of 1991. What type of listening will you need to do when it is read to you? What strategy will help you identify the message?

While a partner reads the passage to you, use your strategy to listen for the facts and details.

Model

from **The Perfect Storm**
by Sebastian Junger

The *Andrea Gail*... [is] seventy-two feet long, has a hull of continuously welded steel plate, and was built in Panama City, Florida, in 1978. She has a 365-horsepower, turbo-charged diesel engine, which is capable of speeds up to twelve knots. There are seven type-one life preservers on board, six Imperial survival suits, a 406-megahertz Emergency Position Indicating Radio Beacon (EPIRB), a 121.5-megahertz EPIRB, and a Givens auto-inflating life raft. There are forty miles of 700-pound test monofilament line on her, thousands of hooks, and room for five tons of bait fish. An ice machine that can make three tons of ice a day sits on her whaleback deck, and state-of-the-art electronics fill her pilothouse: radar, loran, single sideband, VHF, weather track satellite receiver. There's a washer/dryer on board, and the galley has fake wood veneer and a four-burner stove.

> The *Andrea Gail* is one of the biggest moneymakers in Gloucester harbor, and Billy Tyne and Bugsy Moran have driven all the way from Florida to grab sites onboard. The only other sword boat in the harbour that might be able to outfish her is the *Hannah Boden*, skippered by a Colby College graduate named Linda Greenlaw. Not only is Greenlaw one of the only women in the business, she's one of the best captains, period, on the entire East Coast. Year after year, trip after trip, she makes more money than almost anyone else.

Think about It

Read the piece to yourself. How well did your listening strategy work to help you get the information you needed? Was there only one way to listen to this passage? If not, what other way to listen might you use? Why?

Use the Anthology

Practise your listening skills as a partner reads "All I Really Need to Know I Learned in Kindergarten" to you (pages 112-114). Listen to gather content, and listen critically.

Activities

1. When you next give an oral presentation in one of your classes, use signal words or phrases (like "first," "then," "finally"; or "one key point is," "another important thing to know is," "the most important thing is") to help your peers listen more effectively.

2. The next time you're having a conversation with a friend, practise appreciative listening. Then reflect in your reading response journal: How did your ability to listen appreciatively affect your conversation?

3. Practise your listening skills in your next class. Make notes as your teacher talks, listening for key words that highlight major ideas. Later, use your notes to write an outline of the information that was presented.

4. Work with a partner. Choose a short and interesting essay from the anthology, such as "Why Be Polite?" (pages 136-140). Listen critically as your partner reads the essay to you. Then interpret and evaluate the essay.

How to Create an Effective Speaking Style

Before You Start

How we look and how we dress are ways through which we reveal ourselves to others. But often the way we speak — the words, types of sentences, and the tone of voice we use — makes the most lasting impression.

When you write, you have time to choose your words carefully. You can look at them on the page or computer screen and decide whether they are effective and appropriate. When you speak, you also need to take time to choose your words and tone carefully, especially in formal situations when you're making presentations to a variety of audiences. The words you choose can capture and keep your listeners' attention, and the tone you use can give power to your message.

Before you follow the steps to creating an effective speaking style, think about these questions:

- What kinds of presentations do you like listening to? What makes them worth hearing?
- What kinds of oral presentations do you feel most comfortable giving?
- What kinds of language and tone work well for these types of presentations?

Do It Yourself

Step 1 Think about the purpose of your presentation, and note your ideas. What effect do you want to have on your audience? Do you want to:

- inspire them?
- entertain them?
- make them laugh?
- make them think deeply about a serious issue?
- make them feel an emotion?
- make them more knowledgeable?
- challenge their beliefs?
- make them take action?

Ask yourself: What type of language and tone will be effective to help me achieve my purpose?

- **Step 2**   Think about your audience. If they are:
  — your peers; you could use casual or informal language
  — younger than you; use simpler words and sentences
  — older than you; use formal, more complex language

- **Step 3**   Identify what the audience members already know, think, feel, or believe about the topic, like this:
  - "You probably already know _____. But did you realize that ____?"
  - "I know that many of you are secretly worried about what you'll do next year. But think about _____."
  - "Are you one of the 76% of Canadians who believe _____?"

- **Step 4**   Think about ways to reach your audience and make them connect with you, your topic, and your ideas.
  - Tell a story about an experience you've had. Personal stories help your listeners relate to what you're saying. These are sometimes called anecdotes.
  - Use real examples to explain ideas and show how your ideas relate to the real world. Choose examples that will interest your listeners.
  - Use powerful words. Use a thesaurus to help you choose some effective words that will make an impact.
  - Pose a question for the audience to think about — for example, "What would life be like for you if you had no home?" Then paint the picture in words.
  - Help your listeners to "see" what you're saying — for example, "Picture the street in winter… ."
  - Use a variety of sentences to keep your audience's attention. Short sentences can often be more effective than long ones in speeches. Consider using sentence fragments to emphasize a point.
  - Choose and use a quotation that suits the purpose of your presentation.
  - Use facts and details that help to make your case.

- **Step 5** Be as personal in your presentation as is comfortable for you. Tell your audience what you feel about your topic. Use the word "I": "I think," "I feel," "I know," "I believe," "I hope." Being personal gives power to a presentation. People will remember you and what you say.

- **Step 6** Leave your audience with something to remember or think about as you end your presentation. Make an important point, a thought-provoking statement, or end with a meaningful quotation that isn't too long but will stay in the minds of your listeners after you've finished.

HOT tips

- Ask questions. Then follow up with the answers where necessary.
- You can end your presentation with a question to encourage your listeners to keep thinking about the issue or topic — for example, "So what will you do to make the world a better place?"
- Ask rhetorical questions to help engage the minds of your audience. These are the types of questions that don't need an answer — for example, "Who really believes that anymore?"
- Repeat key ideas and points. (People don't remember what they hear as well as they remember what they read or see.) Decide which main ideas are the most important for your audience to remember, and repeat them as a summary or at key moments in your presentation.
- Consider addressing your audience directly (for example, "My friends: we must find a better way ...") once or twice in your presentation. Doing it too often makes you sound as if you are filling up time in your speech.

Making It Work: Language

The following is a welcoming speech from a student council president to new students. What types of sentences do you expect to read in this speech? Why?

Model

Hello, new students! My name is Attiya Joseph, and I'm president of this year's Student Council. It's my job to welcome you to West Carrick Secondary School.

The first thing you should know is that you've just landed in the best school in the city. We're really proud of our school. We're proud of our sports teams. We were provincial champions last year in basketball. We're proud of our arts programs. Many of you are here because you are already artists in music, drama, dance, or visual arts. I'm sure as you got lost in our hallowed halls on your way to this assembly that you saw some of the strange and beautiful art that our Visual Arts students created last year. Our stage band will be playing when we finally let you go to your first class. And don't forget — the Drama Club is having auditions next week. And those are just a few of the amazing opportunities that await you at West Carrick.

I should say a few words about the Student Council before I leave the stage. Your Student Council represents *you*. All your teachers are going to crack the whip because they think the purpose of school is to prepare you for a career, and they're not going to let you forget it! But we, your Student Council, know that school has a more important purpose: it's your social life! Next week we'll be holding elections for class reps to the Council. You'll have to give a speech, but if you win, you'll be on a team of people working to make school enjoyable and fun.

West Carrick's motto is the 3E's: Endeavour, Enterprise, and Excellence. The principal is coming up next to talk to you about all that serious stuff. I want you to remember that your Student Council promises to deliver on the most important part of school — your social life! Together, we'll make your four years here the best.

Thanks, and have a great year.

Think about It

Was your prediction about types of sentences correct? Why is this a good match for the audience? Which punctuation marks in the speech help the speaker to know when to pause and when to emphasize certain words and phrases.

Use the Anthology

Read "The Wealthy Barber" (pages 103-106). Write a speech that you would give to grade seven and eight students to encourage them to save their money. How will you hook their attention at the start of your speech? Make careful choices about the words and sentence structures you use.

Activities

1. Rewrite the student council president's speech in the Model for a different audience. This time, she will give the speech to the parents of new Grade 9 students. How does the language change? How do the sentence structures change? Discuss your observations with your small group.

2. **a.** Work with a partner to write one of the following:
   — a speech you would give in an election to become head of a club or community group
   — a speech you would give about the benefits of doing 40 hours of community service
   — a toast to the bride or groom at their wedding
   — a tribute to your parents or grandparents at a family birthday or anniversary

   b. Rehearse the speech you have written, and have your partner do the same. Deliver the speech to the class or to a small group, and have your partner audiotape or videotape it. Then switch roles. Together, review the tapes and make notes about the things you think you each did well and the areas where you think you could each improve.

3. Choose a print advertisement that uses interesting and effective language. Explain to your partner or small group how the language captures and keeps the attention of the reader.

How to Create and Give Effective Oral Presentations

Before You Start

Speaking skills are important in the world of work. You need them to present yourself well when seeking a job. On the job, you may be asked to speak informally to an individual or a small group (a sales pitch to a customer, a progress report to a committee). You might also need to speak in a more detailed, formal way (giving a presentation or speech at a meeting). In all cases, you want people to listen, so you need to be able to speak confidently and clearly.

Some of the secrets of good presenters are:

- They prepare and organize their presentations.
- They rehearse ahead of time.
- As they speak, they connect with the audience by making eye contact.
- They use body language and gestures to draw attention to key points.
- They use effective volume so everyone can hear, and they use their voices to emphasize what's important.
- They speak at just the right pace.
- They use appropriate and interesting language.
- They use visual aids effectively to highlight key information and ideas, but they don't rely on these to do the job for them.
- They show how they feel.

Before you follow the steps to making an oral presentation, think about these questions:
- What presentations have you had to deliver in class?
- How can good oral presentation skills help you in a job search?
- How can good speaking skills help you in a job interview?

Do It Yourself

Preparing Your Presentation

- **Step 1** Choose a topic for your oral presentation, or use one that your teacher assigns in this or another course. If you are choosing your topic, you will give a better presentation if your topic is one about which you know and care a great deal.

- **Step 2** Consider how you feel, and what you think, about this topic. Is it a serious and important issue? Do you care about it and want others to care too? Do other people understand it? Is it something that people take too seriously? Is it a subject that you find fascinating and want to share with others? In one sentence, explain what the topic means to you.

- **Step 3** Think about the purpose of your presentation. Would others agree with your feelings and thoughts about the topic? How do you want to make the audience feel when they hear your presentation? Some purposes are:

  - to inform your audience: to give them information or ideas
  - to persuade your audience: to change what people believe or feel about a topic or issue
  - to inspire your audience: to make people feel more strongly about a topic or issue
  - to entertain your audience: to make your audience enjoy your treatment of a topic or issue

  Write a sentence that states the purpose of your presentation.

- **Step 4** Plan the content of your presentation. Start by asking yourself questions about the topic. Turn these questions into headings. Write your own ideas and what you already know about the topic. Then do research to complete the information you need: gather information, details, facts, and examples that will answer the questions you've asked yourself about the topic. (See The Stages of the Writing Process, pages 70-73)

- **Step 5** Consider the characteristics of your audience. What is the age of your audience members? What interest do they have in your topic? What might they already know or believe about the topic? What level of language should you use to get and keep their interest? (You may wish to review levels of language on page 126.)

- **Step 6** Organize your research by putting your ideas into the most effective order. Try starting with a strong point and an attention-grabbing example. For each point you make in your presentation, use examples that will appeal to your audience. Save your most important thought for the end to make a lasting impression on your listeners.

- **Step 7** Visuals are effective tools in oral presentations. Some visuals you might use are transparencies, chalk board and flip charts, slides, videotapes, audiotapes, and computer-generated visuals. If you're using statistics or numbers to make a point, try creating a key visual, like a graph or chart, to make the meaning of the statistics clear. Or, use a picture or graphic to create an impression that your words cannot.

Do It Yourself

Presenting

- **Step 1** When you are satisfied with the ideas and the content of your presentation, create an outline to refer to when you speak. Your outline should include the main ideas of your presentation in the order in which you want to present them, as follows:
    1. The topic of your presentation and your purpose in speaking: _____
    2. Main idea: _____
       Key point, fact, detail
       Key point or example
    3. Main idea: _____
       Key point, fact, detail
       Key point or example
    4. Main idea: _____
       Key point, fact, detail
       Key point or example
    5. Ending: Restate your purpose in speaking: _____
       Leave the listeners with an example, story, or quotation that they will remember.

- **Step 2** Do a first rehearsal of your presentation. Use your speaking outline to guide you as you practise speaking in front of an imaginary audience.

Read or speak slowly but naturally. Practise making eye contact, using gestures. (You might want to practise in front of a mirror to judge if your gestures are effective.)

- **Step 3** Practise the tips in step 4. In your next rehearsal, time yourself to judge if you need to change the speed of your delivery. If you plan to use any equipment or visuals during your presentation, practise using them now. Do a final rehearsal in front of a friend or family member. Use his or her feedback to improve your presentation skills.

- **Step 4** Deliver your oral report in front of your intended audience.

  Before presenting
  - Move calmly and quietly to your speaking position.
  - Arrange your material. Place your speaking notes or outline directly in front of you on a speaking stand or table. Arrange your key visuals in their correct order near your speaking notes.
  - Position yourself for speaking. Pause.
  - Make eye contact with the audience.

  While presenting
  - Use your outline or speaking notes to state your purpose.
  - Make eye contact with the audience. Start by looking at someone in the middle of the audience. Then slowly move your eyes across the audience to a person on the left. Return your eyes to the middle, and slowly move your eyes to the right. Continue to maintain eye contact in this way for your whole presentation.
  - Speak clearly and loudly enough to be heard in the back rows.
  - If you move around, move naturally. Don't move too much: it will distract the audience.
  - Let your voice show enthusiasm and appropriate feeling for your topic. Pause to emphasize things that are important.
  - Smile or frown at appropriate places.
  - Use body language and gestures to emphasize your points.

  Ending your presentation
  - Restate the purpose of your presentation and make any other closing remarks.
  - Pause. Hold eye contact with the audience for a few seconds.
  - Wait for the applause.
  - Collect your material and be prepared to answer questions if that is part of the presentation procedure.

> **HOT tips**
> - Always choose a topic or subject that matters to you or is something that you care about. You'll give a more effective presentation if you believe in or are interested in what you're saying.
> - When you're creating your speaking outline, don't write everything in complete sentences. Use point form and only include key words and phrases. Then, when you're speaking, you'll use natural-sounding sentences.
> - Decide if the visuals or media aids you want to use are necessary for your presentation. Be sure you know how to use them, and that everyone can see or hear them.

When Ryan White was 13, he discovered that he'd been infected with the AIDS virus. He acquired the virus through a blood product that he needed to treat his hemophilia, an inherited disease that didn't allow his blood to clot. This is part of his speech to the United States' Presidential Commission on AIDS.

Model

My name is Ryan White. I am 16 years old. I have hemophilia, and I have AIDS.

When I was three days old, the doctors told my parents I was a severe hemophiliac, meaning my blood does not clot. Lucky for me, there was a product just approved by the [U.S.] Food and Drug Administration. It was called Factor VIII, which contains the clotting agent found in blood.

When I was growing up, I had many bleeds or hemorrhages in my joints which were very painful. Twice a week I would receive injections or IVs of Factor VIII which clotted the blood and then broke it down.

The first five to six years of my life were spent in and out of the hospital. All in all I led a pretty normal life.

Most recently my battle has been against AIDS and the discrimination surrounding it. On December 17, 1984, I had surgery to remove 5 cm of my left lung due to pneumonia. After two hours of surgery, the doctors told my mother I had AIDS. I contracted AIDS through my Factor VIII which is made from blood.

I came face to face with death at 13 years old. I was diagnosed with AIDS: a killer. Doctors told me I'm not contagious. Given six months to live and being the fighter that I am, I set high goals for myself. It was my decision to live a normal life, go to school, be with my friends, and enjoy day-to-day activities. It was not going to be easy.

The school I was going to said they had no guidelines for a person with AIDS. The school board, my teachers, and my principal voted to keep me out of the classroom, even after the guidelines were set, for fear of someone getting AIDS from me by casual contact. Rumours of sneezing, kissing, tears, sweat, and saliva spreading AIDS caused people to panic.

We began a series of court battles for nine months, while I was attending classes by telephone. Eventually, I won the right to attend school, but the prejudice was still there. Listening to medical facts was not enough. People wanted 100 percent guarantees. There are no 100 percent guarantees in life, but concessions were made by Mom and me to help ease the fear. We decided to meet everyone halfway:

1. Separate restrooms;
2. No gym;
3. Separate drinking fountain;
4. Disposable eating utensils and trays;

even though we knew that AIDS was not spread through casual contact. Nevertheless, parents of 20 students started their own school. They were still not convinced.

I was labelled a troublemaker, my mom an unfit mother, and I was not welcome anywhere. People would get up and leave so they would not have to sit anywhere near me. Even at church, people would not shake my hand.

It was difficult, at times, to handle, but I tried to ignore the injustice because I knew the people were wrong. My family and I held no hatred for those people because we realized they were victims of their own ignorance. We had great faith that, with patience, understanding, and education, my family and I could be helpful in changing their minds and attitudes around.

My life is better now. At the end of the school year (1986–87), my family and I decided to move to Cicero, Indiana. We did a lot of hoping and praying that the community would welcome us, and they did. For the first time in three years, we feel we have a home, a supportive school, and lots of friends. The communities of Cicero, Atlanta, Arcadia, and Noblesville, Indiana, are now what we call "home." I'm feeling great.

I'm a normal happy teenager again. I have a learner's permit [to drive]. I attend sports functions and dances. My studies are important to me. I made the honour role just recently, with two As and two Bs. I'm just one of the kids, and all because the students at Hamilton Heights High School listened to facts, educated their parents and themselves, and believed in me.

I believe in myself as I look forward to graduating from Hamilton Heights High School in 1991.

Hamilton Heights High School is proof that AIDS education in schools works.

Ryan White died on April 8, 1990, a year before he was to graduate from high school.

Think about It

1. What was the purpose of Ryan White's speech? Would you say that it was more, or less, effective to learn his purpose at the end of the presentation, instead of at the beginning? Why?

2. To make his point, Ryan tells the story of his fight. Explain why sharing personal stories, examples, and anecdotes is particularly effective in presentations.

3. Choose one paragraph of Ryan's speech and focus on the types of sentences he uses. How would you describe these sentences? Why are these appropriate for a speech?

Use the Anthology

Read "A Son's Goodbye" (pages 141-144). Describe the devices that Justin Trudeau uses in his writing to make his speech effective.

Activities

1. Read the essay "Who, Then, Is a "Canadian"?" (pages 10-12). Prepare your own presentation to explain how you feel about being Canadian, using the essay as your guide.

2. Choose one type of visual or media aid that people often use in presentations. Write a set of step-by-step instructions for your peers explaining how to create and use the aid effectively in a presentation. Post your instructions in the classroom as a reference guide.

3. Write the speech that you would give as valedictorian of your graduating class.

How to Communicate in a Group

Before You Start

Employees may work in a group all the time or occasionally, for example to plan and complete a long-term project. Communicating well with others is a key to solving problems well and creating quality products and presentations. It's important to know how to:
— contribute productively to discussions
— help the group set priorities
— record key information from discussions
— decide what information and ideas are useful in solving the problem or completing the task
— summarize discussions and decisions
— report on the group's process for solving the problem or completing the task
— work with the group to complete the task to create quality products and presentations

Before you follow the steps for communicating in a group, think about these questions:
- In what kinds of work do people have to work together every day?
- What important factors have contributed to the success of a group you worked in?
- What have you found to be the most challenging things about working in a group?

Do It Yourself

Communicating in a Group

- **Step 1** Find your role in the group. In groups that work, there are people who:
  - **Initiate** the discussion: they get everyone started.
  - **Encourage**: they ask everyone in the group for their ideas, especially the people who at first don't say much.
  - **Clarify**: they ask others to explain or restate their ideas to make them clearer to everyone.
  - **Summarize**: they restate key ideas so that everyone can agree with the group's direction.
  - **Manage**: they make sure that everyone stays on task; they organize the group's materials and time.

  What roles do you play in a group? Which roles would you like to be better at? Each of the steps that follow will help you to play many key roles in a group and contribute to its success.

- **Step 2** Be sure that you contribute in a helpful way to discussions.

  To make sure that all group members have a chance to share their ideas, establish an order for speaking in the group. If you don't have an idea when it's your turn, just say "Pass." When you do have an idea, or you want to respond to another idea, raise your hand or use a signal agreed on by the group. (You can write your idea, then state it when your turn comes.)

  Each time the group meets, choose someone to conduct the discussion. That person makes sure that everyone has a chance to speak.

- **Step 3** Help the group set priorities. First, discuss what tasks are important to accomplish. List these tasks, then order them from the most important to the least important. With your group, plan how to do the work.

- **Step 4** Choose someone to record key information as the group discusses and makes decisions. The recorder should use a variety of ways to make notes. Visual and graphic organizers are a good way of recording and relating information and ideas. At the first stage of discussion, the recorder should record every idea that is suggested.

Making It Work: Language

- **Step 5** Help the group assess information and ideas. When the ideas have been recorded, everyone in the group should have a second look at the information to decide if it is useful and necessary to the task. The recorder should read back each idea to the group. The group will then decide whether to keep the idea, modify it, discard it, or add a new one. Do this until all the ideas have been assessed.
- **Step 6** Once the key ideas have been chosen or decisions have been made, each member of the group should write a brief summary of the important information that was discussed and the decisions the group has made.
- **Step 7** At the end of each group session, one member of the group should report to the teacher, employer, or manager about the group's progress in solving the problem or completing the task. Do this face to face or in a written report.

Hot tips

- Don't shut down discussion with comments like, "That won't work" or "We've already tried that" or "That's a stupid idea." Say instead, "That's interesting. Does anyone have a different idea?" Keep ideas flowing.
- When someone in your group is dominating the discussion, turn to another person and ask him or her for an idea.
- If there are too many people talking at once, encourage everyone to take a few minutes to write down their ideas. Then hear everyone in turn.

Do It Yourself

Creating High-Quality Products and Presentations

- **Step 1** As a group, discuss your final product. Consider:
  - what form it will take (brochure, report, multi-media presentation, visual display)
  - how long it should be (number of pages, number of minutes, how many visuals and their size)
  - the types and amount of information it should contain (number of subtopics to research, what issues it will address, how much evidence should be used to support opinions and issues)
  - the final deadline for finishing it

- **Step 2** Discuss your group members' individual interests, strengths, and skills. Divide the research tasks among all members of the group so that all topics and subtopics have been assigned.
- **Step 3** Use your research skills to find and record the information, ideas, and evidence that are required to complete your part of the task.
- **Step 4** Meet as a group to share information orally. Select one person in the group to make an outline of the group's researched information and ideas.
- **Step 5** As a group, decide on the most effective order for the researched information. For example, to capture your audience's attention in a report on Worker Health and Safety, you might begin the report with statistics about accidents on the job.
- **Step 6** All members of the group write a first draft or create a first version of their section of the product and then shares this version with a peer reviewer. This is a good time to add any needed information, delete anything that is unnecessary, or change the order of ideas. This will result in a new draft or version of each section of the product.
- **Step 7** Put the revised sections in order to create a draft of your group's work. Edit your draft by conferring with peers or by using dictionaries, thesauruses, and computer editing software to make your draft accurate and effective.
- **Step 8** Make design decisions with your group about the final product. As a group, create a paper and pencil "mock-up" of the design to show the layout of your product. Decide what illustrations and graphics will make the final product effective. Then divide the remaining tasks among the group members.
- **Step 9** Use a word-processing program or other computer software to incorporate the design elements and to publish the group's product.

Hot tips

- Understand your own role and responsibilities in the group. If you don't, ask someone for clarification.
- When you volunteer for a task, make sure that you have the skills you need to accomplish it.
- Appreciate the efforts of others.
- Consult manuals and instructions to help you understand how to use publishing software.

In this scenario, three people have agreed to work together on a task. They are sharing the research part of the task, but each person has also taken a special role. Why is it a good idea for everyone to share some work equally? What are the advantages to the group if people take on special roles?

Model

Ahmed, Maria, and Russell are going to work together to create a one-page fact sheet about a special event to be held in their community. The fact sheet will be used to advertise the community event in the local newspaper, and will also be part of the posters to be displayed. The group must do the following:
- research the community event
- make notes, and organize, draft, revise and edit the information
- decide on accompanying visuals and graphics
- create an effective layout
- produce the final copy for the community event.

Each of them will conduct research by interviewing the leaders of many community organizations that will be hosting the event. In addition, each has agreed to take responsibility for one aspect of the work.
- Maria will be the Group Manager. She will find the names and phone numbers of the community leaders that the group members will contact. She will remind the group of time limits and will keep everyone on task.
- Russell will be the Group Recorder. When the group finds its information, he will record the information for the group.
- Ahmed will be the Group Designer of the fact sheet. He will create the design, graphics, and illustrations that the group decides to use in the fact sheet.

Think about It

What skills would you need to fulfil each role listed in the Model? Why are these skills important to a group? Which of the roles listed in the Model appeals to you the most? What skills do you have that would help you take on that role effectively?

Use the Anthology

Read "Working for You" (pages 173-175). Work in a group to research similar employee benefits for two or three other Canadian companies. Create a presentation to compare the benefits packages.

Activities

1. Work in a group to create a one-page fact sheet about a career that interests all group members.

2. Use the step-by-step instructions on pages 158-159 to create a report, a brochure, or a multi-media presentation on a topic that interests your group.

How to Create Your Own Voice in Writing

Before You Start

We can usually recognize the voice of someone we know when we hear it on the telephone or from across a crowded room. We each have a unique voice when we speak. We also have a unique voice when we write. That voice or style is created by the words we choose, the types of sentences that we use, how we put our sentences together, and the topics and themes that we usually write about. Our speaking voice conveys a tone and feelings to our reader. Our writing voice does, too.

Before you follow the steps to creating your own voice in writing, think about these questions:
- What is style? How would you describe your own fashion style or the style of music you like most?
- Describe a style of writing you enjoy reading, and explain why you like it.

Do It Yourself

Steps

- **Step 1** Focus on your **word choice**. The words you choose are the most important factor in creating your writer's voice. They create the tone and mood in your writing. Imagine that you are using words to paint a word picture that will make your reader see, think, and feel your meaning.
  - Decide what your purpose is for writing. For example, if you want to make your audience feel passionately about an issue, use words that you think will move your audience.
  - Think about who will be reading your piece and what kind of language they are most likely to respond to.
  - Use a thesaurus to help you choose the most effective words.

Step 2 Decide on the **tone of voice** you want in your writing. You can create many different kinds of tones, for example serious, humorous, casual, confidential, and romantic.
- Choose the appropriate level of language to suit your audience and purpose. For example, use simpler language for children than for your peers or an adult audience, and use slang or colloquial language when addressing your peers, but not a community leader.

If you want to create a **formal** tone:
— think of your reader as someone who is educated and knowledgeable.
— use words that are clear and precise in their meaning.
— appeal to the reader with argument, support, and logic.
— use complete sentences.
— avoid using dashes and exclamation marks.

If you want to create an **informal** tone:
— think of your reader as someone with whom you might have an informal conversation.
— choose words that will have special meaning for the reader.
— appeal to a wide range of emotions, beliefs, thoughts, and judgements that the reader might have.
— use less formal sentence structure and less complex sentences.
— use punctuation effectively to make your writing sound more like spoken language.

Step 3 Use effective **literary devices** to create a strong voice and style in your writing. You might choose some of the devices below.
- When you are describing, use images and imagery to create a picture.
- When you want to make a comparison, use simile, metaphor, or personification.
- When your speaker has the same knowledge and experiences that you do, use allusions.
- When you want to involve the reader and have the reader think with you, use rhetorical questions.
- When you want to say one thing when you really mean another, use irony.

This is an excerpt from a speech made by Sir John A. Macdonald in 1865. In this speech, he is trying to convince members of other provinces to join together in confederation to create the Dominion of Canada. When you read Macdonald's speech, take note of the types of words and sentences he uses and how he uses punctuation. How do these work together to create a formal tone?

Model 1

Let me again, before I sit down, impress upon this House the necessity of meeting this question in a spirit of compromise, with a disposition to judge the matter as a whole, to consider whether really it is for the benefit and advantage of the country to form a Confederation of all the provinces; and if honourable gentlemen, whatever may have been their conceived ideas as to the merits of the details of this measure, whatever may still be their opinions as to these details, if they really believe that the scheme is one by which the prosperity of the country will be increased, and its future progress secured, I ask them to yield their own views, and to deal with the scheme according to its merits as one great whole.

The following example of informal English uses the type of language we most often read in newspapers, magazines, and other publications that have a wide reading audience. As you read the passage, take note of the words, phrases, types of sentences, and punctuation the writer uses. How do these help to create an informal tone?

Model 2

Minding Their Own Business
Toronto Star, Monday, March 4, 2001

After a few flops with the formula, the designers of a new bubble bath finally have a recipe that works and are sketching out their marketing plan.

With the product set to be launched at a spring trade show, this is a busy season for the pair of budding moguls. Plus there's all their other grade 8 homework.

Bubble bath bosses S.L. and L.F. are part of an unusual program that teaches the basics of business — from sales to safety — to children in grades 7 and 8.

Students accepted into the special stream take an extra business class and a special business computer lab each day and tackle hands-on projects, from designing and launching their own product to running a hot dog stand and managing a café.

"I thought the program might be more for computer geeks, but it's actually lots of fun and prepares you so much for high school," S. said, holding a gift-wrapped sample of bath balm — or their "Product Prototype with Packaging."

"But it's major time management in this program because of the extra courses. At times there can be five hours of homework a night."

In deciding which product to make, the girls researched the products sold at last year's in-school trade show to avoid any glut in the market.

"Chocolate and candy; there was so much of those last year that we decided bubble bath would be better for our target market of girls our age and guys buying for their mothers."

Students in the program must "shadow" a working person for a day, perform five hours of community service, and help run a one-day hot-dog stand and a French-style café.

When we echo in our writing the type of language we use while speaking to our peers, we are using colloquial English. Examine the sample of colloquial speech below. Take note of the types of words and phrases, sentence structure, and punctuation that the author uses. How do these work together to create a casual and familiar tone?

Model 3

A Typical Teenager

I am a typical teenager. At least I would like to be. My secret ambition is to go to a Caribbean island and surf, tan, and hang out. I like cool stuff like fab clothes … right now everyone's into brand name T-shirts and capris. And I love to dance. I wear my hair in the latest style and to keep it looking full and fluffy I have extensions added to my own hair.

Think about It

Make a comparison chart to summarize how each model uses language differently. Compare the type of words and phrases, sentence structure, and punctuation that each model uses.

Use the Anthology

From *Moving On*, find selections that are an example of the use of: a formal tone, an informal tone, and colloquial language. Make an inference about each writer's intended audience. Then discuss your conclusions with a small group.

Activities

1. Select a piece of your own writing that you like. Analyze your writing style in the piece — the words you use, your tone, your sentence structure, how you use punctuation, how you use literary devices. Then describe your writer's voice.

2. Locate from a variety of outside sources (magazines, newspapers, ads) samples of the three levels of language (see page 126). Clip and display samples of formal, informal, and colloquial language. Explain what level of language the writer used and why he or she chose to present their ideas in that way.

3. Write two short pieces of text. Title one Mad Talking and the other Smooth Talking. In the texts, explain to readers how you talk "mad" and how you talk "smooth." What is different about how you used language in each piece?

4. To welcome a relative or good friend who has just moved to your neighbourhood, you plan to introduce him or her to three groups of people. Write the different introductions you would make when introducing the newcomer to your classmates, a group of teachers, and the members of your sports team.

    In each case think of the language and tone you'd use with your audience. How would your introductions be different for each audience?

Media

TABLE OF CONTENTS

Make the Connection	168
How to Assess Information from Media	170
How to Describe Design and Production Choices in Media	174
How to Identify Bias in Visual, Auditory, and Print Media	178
How to Understand and Analyze Audience Reaction	182
How to Create a Radio Commercial	186
How to Create a Photo Essay	189

Make the Connection

"Whoever controls the media – the images – controls the culture."
—Allen Ginsberg

▸ What we need to know about media

Many of us hear the word "media" a lot. What is media? "Media" is the plural of the word "medium". A medium is the means by which a message is sent from producer to consumer (for example, radio, newspaper, film). When people talk about media, they are usually talking about mass media — ways in which information is communicated to a lot of people (or a mass of people) at once. There are six main areas of media:

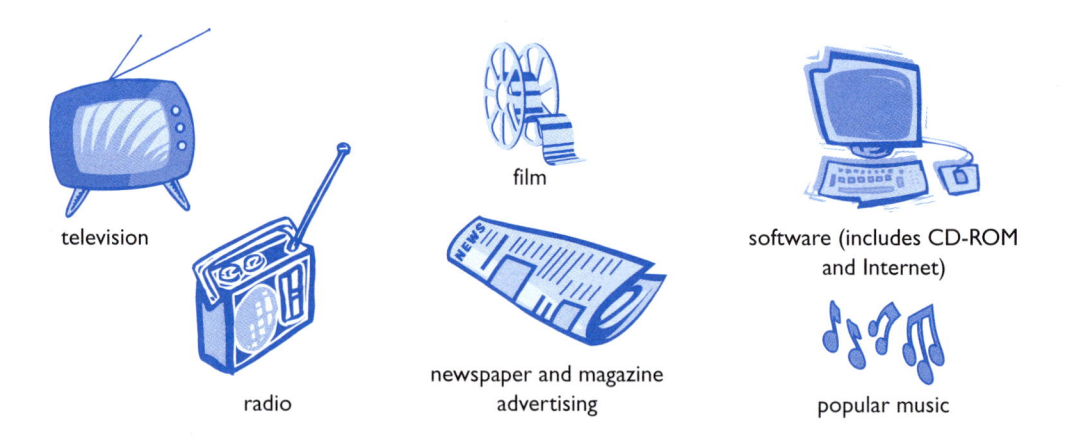

- television
- radio
- film
- newspaper and magazine advertising
- software (includes CD-ROM and Internet)
- popular music

Over time, forms of mass media have changed.

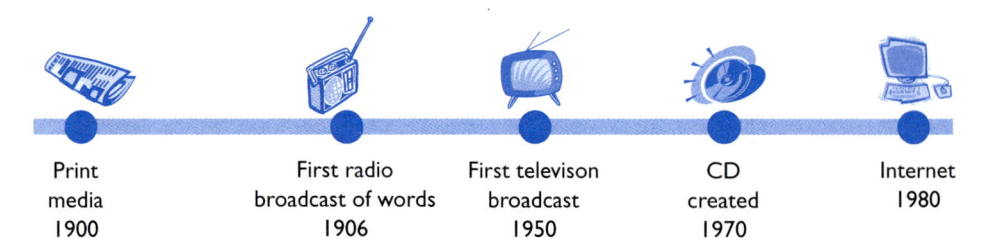

| Print media 1900 | First radio broadcast of words 1906 | First televison broadcast 1950 | CD created 1970 | Internet 1980 |

▶ The message of media

Because we are constantly exposed to them, media affect our lives and influence the way we think and act. In your notebook, create a seven-column chart with a heading for each day of the week. Identify how much time each day you spend listening to music on CDs, watching television, listening to a radio station, or using the Internet. Compare weekdays and weekends. What differences do you notice? Which form of media do you think influences you most? Why?

The messages in media are always around us; we need to learn to view media critically so that we are aware of the messages they send. In this unit, you will learn techniques for viewing media critically, for identifying bias in media, and for creating various media. As you work with media in this unit, keep your chart and your analysis with you so that you continue to be aware of how the messages of media affect you.

How to Assess Information from Media

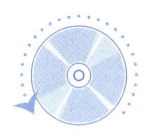

Before You Start

People who produce media make many choices and decisions as they put together the images they want to pass on to the consumer. As a consumer, you need to learn how to identify these messages and figure out how valid they are. There are two levels to every image in most media:

— the basic, or **literal**, level is the image that the producer selects

— the **affective** level is the reaction the image creates in you

To take apart a media message, you need to think about the meaning being conveyed on both levels of the image. Imagine an image of a teenage girl crying. Her hair is messy, her clothes are torn, there is fear in her eyes. The producer has selected that image to send a certain message. As a consumer, you need to think about why the producer selected that image. At the same time, the image causes a reaction in you. You need to reflect on your own reaction, and be sure that you are not being manipulated or influenced without realizing it.

Before you follow the steps to assessing information from media, think about these questions:

- What media representations (ads, television shows, and so on) have you enjoyed? Why?
- What media representations have made you angry? Why?
- What techniques were used in media representations that you have enjoyed? Have not enjoyed?

Do It Yourself

- **Step 1** View or listen to a media representation of your choice or one that your teacher assigns. Make notes of your findings and observations.
- **Step 2** Use the questions in the steps that follow to assess the meaning behind what you see or hear.

How to Assess Information from Media

Step 3 For a news report, think about the point of view. Consider:
- Does a news report give you more than just the facts? How? Why? Does it make you feel a certain way?
- Is there more than one view explained in the information?
- How is this information given by other media outlets?
- Are there visuals that accompany the information? How do the visuals make you feel? Do they change how you might feel if you read or heard only the words?

Step 4 For advertising, think about whether there are hidden messages in the media representation. Consider:
- What is being done to attract your attention?
- Is a product associated with a particular group of people? Is this to convince you that the product can make you similar to that group? Why?
- Do the images relate to the product, or do the images have a message of their own?

Step 5 Think about whether the message of the news report or ad makes sense based on what you believe. Consider:
- Is this an accurate portrayal of what you honestly know to be true about these facts or this product?
- Are the visual images accurate?
- Are the words used an honest representation of the situation?
- Does the information make sense to you as a Canadian (for example, does it focus on American holidays, the American system of government, and so on)?

Step 6 Use your notes to write a brief analysis of the media representation. Your analysis should identify the media piece and where you found it, the topic, the information you have received from the media piece (based on your answers to the questions), and what the producer has done to convey that information.

Making It Work: Media

HOT tips

- Be aware of media trying to go beyond the facts of a story to make you feel a certain way about the story.
- Be aware of hidden messages that may try to convince you to feel a certain way.
- Understand that some messages may offer only American attitudes and traditions and may be not be relevant to the Canadian experience.

What is the first thing you notice about this ad?

Model

Community Sports ...
BECAUSE EVERY KID DESERVES A SHOT.

With this year's community sports program, local kids had a safe place to play, learned the value of teamwork, and felt great about themselves. Thank you for playing a part.

Your Community Sports Association
WORKING TOGETHER... PLAYING TOGETHER

Think about It

Discuss with a partner the explicit information and the implicit information you were able to get from this ad. Give details from the ad to support your comments.

Use the Anthology

View the ad "In a year when so much was taken …" (pages 32-33). Follow the steps on pages 170–171 of this handbook to assess the information you can gather from the ad. Share your findings with a small group.

Activities

1. A newspaper is covering a story about teenagers looking for part-time work. The teenager chosen for the interview was found at the mall, is dressed in extreme punk fashion, and makes negative comments about working part-time. This article is placed on the second page of the newspaper and is read mostly by adult readers. Analyze the conclusion that the reader may make about teens, how they dress, and their attitude to work. Determine whether the editor has been fair to teens. What would you do about this?

2. Is your favourite sitcom, daytime soap, or movie American in content? If so, in groups, discuss what changes you would need to make to ensure that the content of the show is clearly Canadian. If not, in groups, discuss what changes would be needed to ensure that the show's content is clearly American.

3. Imagine that you want to purchase a dog or cat. Do an Internet search on the breed of your choice. Which sites listed do you think would have the most accurate information. Why? List the five sites you would visit first, in order of appeal, then visit each one. Explain and describe to a partner whether each site met your expectations and provided you with the information necessary to make a decision about purchasing an animal.

How to Describe Design and Production Choices in Media

Before You Start

Media representations are designed to send a message to the consumer. A company may hire someone to create various media: an instructional video to help train new employees; an ad to sell a product on television, radio, or in print; a Web site to advertise the company and sell its products, and so on. The media producer must consider carefully the audience to whom the ads are directed and ensure that the audience gets the message the company wants to send.

Different media send messages in different ways. A producer must convey messages that are powerful and make their point quickly and memorably. Use of colour, music, and language, and an appeal to the audience's age group, cultural group, and gender add power and voice to the message.

Before you follow the steps to describing design and production choices in media, think about these questions:
- What radio stations, television programs, magazines, and Web sites appeal to you?
- How do your parents' or younger/older siblings' choices of the above types of media differ from yours? Why?

Do It Yourself

Step 1 View a media representation, such as a music video, a display ad, a television show, or a magazine of your choice or one that your teacher assigns. Take notes as you work through each of the following steps.

- **Step 2** Identify the target audience. There are several ways to classify an audience. For example:
  — by its work status
  — by the audience's view of itself
  — by its social grouping (gender, age, culture, marital status, class)
  — by its social position (education, religion, rural vs. urban, geographical region)

  Using Steps 3, 4, and 5 will help you find clues to identify the target audience.

- **Step 3** Notice the language that is used. How do the characters speak? What language is used to describe the product, information, or characters? Why was this language chosen?

- **Step 4** Identify how colour is used. Certain colours are symbolic of certain traits, and producers use colours to send a message (for example, a yellow door may send the message to be cautious of opening it; a figure dressed all in black may signal fear). These are some examples of what colours may traditionally represent:
  — Black: power, anger, night, death, magic, formality
  — Red: passion, love, daring, excitement, action
  — Green: youth, freshness, rebirth, healing, life, growth
  — Blue: clarity, truth, honesty, tranquillity, spirituality
  — Yellow: caution, positive attitude, intellectualism
  — Orange: ambition, self-sufficiency, joy
  — Brown: warmth, earthiness, comfort, familiarity, hard-working, conscientious

- **Step 5** Identify how music is used. What background or theme music is included? How does it manipulate the emotions of the audience? How do the lyrics relate to the action?

- **Step 6** Identify the appeal to a Canadian audience. What makes the media representation Canadian? What makes it not related to the Canadian experience?

- **Step 7** Write an analysis based on your responses. Name the type of media, the title (if any), and where you found the media representation. Then list the design or production choices that the producer made, and support your ideas with details from the media representation.

176 | Making It Work: Media

HOT tips

- Think about the connotations of words and images in the media representations you analyze, and what message the designer or producer is sending with the choice of a particular word or image.

What is your first impression of the CD cover below?

Model

CD cover: **HOME** — The Rae Sharman Band

- black and white cover
- one-word title
- large, single image
- small type used for band name

Think about It

Explain why you think the creator of the CD cover made the choices indicated in the model (page 176).

Use the Anthology

Read "I Volunteer" (pages 70-73). Write several paragraphs to describe the design choices made by the creator and to explain the effect of each choice. Consider such elements as colour, font choice, type style, layout, and visuals.

Activities

1. Collect four different magazines, two that are Canadian in content and two that are American in content. From the four magazines select two ads, one for a Canadian product, company, or service, and one for an American product, company, or service.

    Use the steps on pages 174-175 to analyze the advertisers' message. Create a chart for comparison.

2. In groups, discuss the colours that are linked to particular rock groups, teenage social groups, or specific celebrities. What message does the colour use send?

3. With a group, brainstorm the uniform or signage colours for a variety of fast-food restaurants. Then discuss what message the company is trying to send.

4. Write an analysis of the design or production choices for the last movie you saw, your current favourite music video, or your favourite television program.

How to Identify Bias in Visual, Auditory, and Print Media

Before You Start

A bias is an inclination or preference. Media sources do not always present issues fairly, but their bias is not always obvious. Media formats may show bias through a stereotype, or a simplified image of a group in society. (On television, viewers may see stereotypical characters such as the rebellious teen or the ruthless businessperson.) Stereotypes are often used to give information quickly.

Use of stereotypes may make viewers forget that people are more complicated than the stereotype can convey.

News media are expected to be objective—to report only facts. But bias appears in news media. We expect bias in an editorial, for instance, where an editor gives facts then shares an opinion on them. However, news media may have a bias that is less obvious to the consumer. For example, they may target their information to certain groups (blue-collar workers, business people) or report more heavily on local over international issues. Comparing and contrasting different sources on similar issues can help you identify their biases.

Learn to be a critical viewer and to question the images that you see in various forms of media.

Before you follow the steps to identifying bias in media, think about these questions:

- What ads have you seen that stereotype a group, such as the elderly? What conclusions did you draw about the group during the ad?
- What stereotypes of teenagers have you seen that you know to be untrue of teenagers?
- What dangers can come from drawing conclusions about a group based on a stereotype?

How to Identify Bias in Visual, Auditory, and Print Media

Do It Yourself

Steps

- **Step 1** Choose a media representation to analyze for bias, or analyze one that your teacher assigns. Make notes of your findings and observations.

- **Step 2** To identify bias in visual or auditory media (television, films, commercials, radio), answer the following questions:

  1. Who or what is being represented?
  2. Is the representation fact or opinion? How do you know?
  3. Who made this representation? Is it realistic or imaginary?
  4. What is the first message you notice? How is it conveyed?
  5. How are the people or objects represented? Are there stereotypes?
  6. Why did the producer choose this image or series of images?
  7. Is it fair, and presented in a balanced way, or can you see some signs of bias?
  8. What can you relate the representation to in your own life?

- **Step 3** To identify bias in publications, ask yourself the following:

  1. What is the publication's view on the issue? What facts support the view?
  2. Does the publication represent the issue in a balanced way? Are there conflicting views that are not included?
  3. Do the sources used represent a variety of cultures? A balance of male and female viewpoints? A variety of political viewpoints?
  4. Are people of different ages, races, genders, physical abilities, family structures, appearances, and socio-economic levels involved in the same actions treated in the same way?
  5. Do the headlines accurately reflect the content of the stories, or is the headline misleading? (For example, does a headline make a story sound more emotional than it is?)
  6. What issues appear on the front page or close to the front? What issues appear near the back of the paper? How is this significant?
  7. Do front-page photos and other key photos support the content of articles, or are they misleading? (For example, are the photos more dramatic than the text?)

- **Step 4** Think about what techniques the media producer has used (such as images, sounds, colours, humour, print style) to get and hold the audience's attention. List them in your reading response journal.

Making It Work: Media

> **Step 5** Use your notes to write an analysis of bias in this media representation. Your analysis should identify the media piece and where you found it, the topic, how the topic is treated (based on your answers to the questions), and what bias, if any, that treatment shows.

H●T tips
- Ask questions about the choices a media producer makes when trying to convey a message to an audience. This can help you identify bias, and help you make up your own mind about what you are listening to, seeing, or reading.
- You can apply these questions to other types of media. The key is to think critically about the message and how it is being sent.

Read only the headline of the following article. Write a sentence describing what you expect the article to be about.

Model

CANADIAN FAILS TO WIN GOLD

SALT LAKE CITY Canadian cross-country skier Beckie Scott pulled out all the stops yesterday afternoon to push her way onto the medal podium and earn Canada's first bronze medal of these games.

Think about It

Was your prediction correct? What bias did the headline show? Write an alternative headline for the article.

Use the Anthology

Choose a newspaper or magazine article from *Moving On*. Use the steps on pages 179-180 of this handbook to help you identify, and analyze, any bias shown in the article.

Activities

1. Find a show on television that deals with a family situation. Does this family look like your family or anyone's family that you know? What is different about the "television family" compared to a real family? Why are these images presented in this way?

2. Choose three different newspapers. Read the front page of each paper for three days. Compare the front pages of the three papers. What differences do you see reflected in the front page of each paper? Use the steps on pages 179-180 of this handbook to determine bias for each paper. What conclusion can you draw by analyzing the content of the front page of each paper?

How to Understand and Analyze Audience Reaction

Before You Start

The audience is the most important part of the economics of the media. The choices that consumers make strongly influence producers. For example, movie theatres book top-grossing films to continue to draw a large paying audience. A film that has been released and is being rejected by the viewing audience will often be pulled from the theatres and moved into the video market. In the workplace, companies make product or marketing decisions based on the way an audience reacts to surveys, presentations, products, and so on.

Advertisers divide audiences into target markets or groups to whom they want to sell. Advertisers conduct in-depth research, or data mining, to learn about the preferences, routines, and lifestyles of their audiences, then use this information to determine when and through which media to advertise their products.

Before you follow the steps to understanding and analyzing audience reaction, think about these questions:
- Why is the reaction of an audience so important to a media producer?
- What type of audience reaction do you look for when you make a presentation? What changes might you make based on that reaction?

Do It Yourself

Steps

● **Step 1** Understand how to identify an audience. Here are some of the categories into which media producers divide the audience.

1. Work status
   - A: higher management/professional
   - B: middle management/administration/ professional
   - C1: junior management/supervisory/professional
   - C2: skilled manual
   - D: semi-skilled/unskilled
   - E: unemployed/casual worker/pensioner

2. How the audience members see themselves
   Succeeders: think of themselves as powerful and in control
   Aspirers: want a better life
   Carers: have a social conscience
   Mainstreamers: prefer to be like most other people
   Individualists: prefer to be different from most people

3. Social group (John Hartley, *Understanding News*, 1982)
   self
   family
   gender
   class
   age group
   nation and ethnicity

4. Social position (John Fiske, *Television Culture*, 1987)
   education
   region
   religion
   urban or rural background
   political allegiance

Step 2 Prepare a media representation for delivery to a target audience. Before you begin, note everything you know about the audience. You might:
- give an oral presentation
- observe an audience during the viewing of a media representation
- do a survey on a topic or product of your choice or one assigned by your teacher.

You may wish to work with a partner to analyze the reaction of your audience. One of you can deliver the media representation, while the other takes notes on his or her observations of the audience. You can switch roles when repeating the activity at another time.

> **Step 3** Consider the data you and your partner have gathered. Write notes to answer the following:
> - Who is the audience?
> - Is there more than one group in the audience? Define each.
> - What emotional responses did the audience show (laughter, interest, boredom, anger, agreement, understanding, and so on)?
> - What did the audience like? Dislike?
>
> **Step 4** With your partner, write an analysis of the audience, using your notes from Step 3. Include, as well, any information about changes you would make to your representation as a result of the audience's reaction.

HOT tips

- You can figure out the audience of a given media source by focussing on its advertising for a given time period. Listen to the ads on a radio station during a one-hour period, or view the ads in a single section of a newspaper. List the products or services advertised. How are they the same? What type of person might be interested in those products or services?

Read the title, description, and time slot of the television show below. Whom do you think the target market might be?

Model

Hot on the Trail — detective drama, 1 hour, Tuesday 9 pm

Air time sold to:
DRB Wireless Communications — Keeping you in touch
Silenza — The elegant sports car for the way you live today
MyBank — A mortgage designed to make you comfortable
Hall of Fame Televison Drama
Cool Cola — All taste, no calories
QuickDry — The dry-cleaning alternative

Think about It

After reading which companies advertise during the television show, do you think your prediction about its target audience was correct? Why does the advertising suit the show's viewers?

Use the Anthology

Read "Television Viewing: The Human Dimension" (pages 28-31). Write a brief statement to summarize what it says about audiences.

Activities

1. a. Think of your three favourite television shows. List as many characteristics as you can that might describe the target audience of each. Organize the list into the three key features that identify that audience. In groups, determine if there was one or more favourite show that each group member identified. If there was, compare your analysis of each show's audiences. Discuss the main elements that demonstrate how the show's creators purposely directed the content to a particular group.

   b. Are the characters in the show employed? Identify their employment. Does the work the characters do reflect the lifestyle they live?

2. Define the term "data mining." Explain what data mining is used for and why it would be important to advertisers and others who need to take into account audience reaction.

How to Create a Radio Commercial

Before You Start

Radio continues to evolve and remains a major form of media. Many radio stations now broadcast onto the Internet and have a worldwide rather than a local, provincial, or even national, audience.

A company that wants to advertise on the radio buys a certain amount of air time from the station. Since the listener can only hear (not see) the product or service, radio ads have to catch a listener's attention with only sound. Messages must be geared to the specific audience, and must be short, simple, and creative. Radio ads are usually 30 or 60 seconds long.

Before you follow the steps to creating a radio commercial, think about these questions:

- What radio station do you listen to most? Who is that station's target audience? What kinds of ads do you hear on this station?
- What radio commercials catch your attention? Why do you think that is?
- Why might someone choose to advertise on the radio instead of through a visual medium?

Do It Yourself

Steps

- **Step 1** Choose a product or service to advertise on your radio commercial, or use one assigned by your teacher.

- **Step 2** Identify your audience and when that audience is most likely to be listening to the radio. What will the station be broadcasting before and following your commercial? In general, the programming on a radio station falls into two categories:

    1. Foreground: This format encourages active listening and includes news shows, talk shows, radio theatre, phone-in shows, and so on.

    2. Background: This is a music-programming format that is designed to be in the background while the listener is engaged in another activity. It is not intended to be central to a listener's focus.

How to Create a Radio Commercial

- **Step 3** Decide how you will get the attention of your audience. Begin your script by writing a strong slogan or opening line.
- **Step 4** Write body copy for your ad to create an interest in, or desire for, your product or service. Be sure to include all key information that your audience will need to make a decision and to choose your product or service. Decide whether to use one voice or more than one voice. Decide whether your body copy will be a monologue or a dialogue.

  If you wish, include a promotion or special feature in your commercial.
- **Step 5** Write a strong closing to your ad that identifies your product or service and what makes it special.
- **Step 6** Think of how you can use music and sound effects to enhance the message of your ad. Add these to your radio script.

Hot tips

- Research shows that teenage audiences are drawn to products promoted by music celebrities.
- Prime time for radio listeners is 7:00 to 9:00 a.m., and 4:00 to 6:00 p.m.

The following is a script for a radio commercial. What challenges, if any, do you expect to encounter when you read it?

Model

Radio Commercial

(Telephone ringing)

Female voice: Good afternoon, Reva Manufacturing. (pause) Oh, I'm sorry, that position is filled. Thank you for calling. (Clicking sound of telephone hanging up)

(Telephone ringing)

Male voice: Good morning, thank you for calling Holmes. (pause) No, I'm sorry we're not hiring at this time. Have a good day. (Clicking sound of telephone hanging up)

Making It Work: Media

> (Telephone ringing)
> Male voice: Hello, and thank you for calling Boxtops, your local recycler. How may I direct your call? (pause) No, that position is no longer available. Good luck, though. (Clicking sound of telephone hanging up)
> V/O: Tired of the hang-ups when you call about a job? Then it's time for you to visit us at XYZ Job Training. We'll teach you how to find the hidden jobs, how to be the first to apply for them, and how to get the job that's right for you. Call us today at (808) 555-1XYZ, or find us online at www.xyztraining.ca.
> V/O: XYZ Job Training — the right job, that's right for you.

Think about It

What information can you gather from reading this radio commercial script? Have a partner read it aloud. What additional information can you gather, if any, from listening?

Use the Anthology

Using any short story or play in *Moving On*, identify the target audience, and create a product and a radio commercial that would appeal to that audience.

Activities

1. Listen to a commercial on your favourite radio station. Do you think the commercial targets you, as a radio listener, well? Did it attract and keep your attention and give you all the information you needed? Explain your answer.

2. Create a radio commercial to appeal to a teenage or young adult audience. Now adapt the commercial to suit two completely different target audiences. Audiotape your commercials and share them with the class.

How to Create a Photo Essay

Before You Start

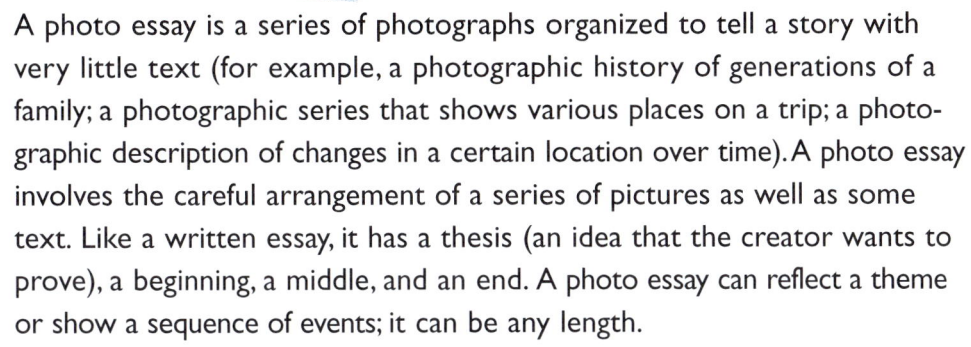

A photo essay is a series of photographs organized to tell a story with very little text (for example, a photographic history of generations of a family; a photographic series that shows various places on a trip; a photographic description of changes in a certain location over time). A photo essay involves the careful arrangement of a series of pictures as well as some text. Like a written essay, it has a thesis (an idea that the creator wants to prove), a beginning, a middle, and an end. A photo essay can reflect a theme or show a sequence of events; it can be any length.

Before you follow the steps to creating a photo essay, think about these questions:

- Where might you find a photo essay?
- Why might you want to create a photo essay?
- What advantages does a photo essay have over a written essay?

Do It Yourself

- **Step 1** Choose a topic for your photo essay, or use a topic assigned by your teacher.
- **Step 2** Research your topic by visiting the location of the shoot, meeting any people involved, and so on. Get the cooperation of any people whose photographs you are taking, or who can help you get access to certain locations that you want to photograph. If you are photographing children, have their parent or guardian sign a release form that allows you to exhibit or publish the photographs.

Steps

- **Step 3** Plan your photo shoot from beginning to end, making clear, descriptive notes. You might also find it useful to create a storyboard for your photo shoot. You will want to consider:

  - an establishing shot that sets the scene
  - a beginning, a middle, and an end to your essay
  - what kinds of pictures you need, and what images you want to include
  - the viewpoints, perspective, and details you want to include to complete the essay

- **Step 4** Be sure you have all of your equipment, and begin shooting your story. You will need to take many shots to get the outcome you want. A digital camera will allow you to take and store many shots until you have the right ones. If you are using a 35mm camera, bring at least three rolls of film so you have many photos to choose from.

  Use your storyboard as a guide, allowing the story to unfold. You may revise some of your ideas as the story begins to reveal itself.

- **Step 5** Develop the pictures. If you are using a 35mm camera, create a contact sheet, which is a sheet of proofs of the photographs. This is an inexpensive way of viewing your shots before committing to developing the ones you will use. If you are using a digital camera, print out all the pictures you took. Look through the proofs and choose the pictures that best tell the story.

- **Step 6** Assemble your photo essay. Remember to include the establishing photo that sets the tone, and a solid completion photo that pulls the essay together. Add written captions if you wish.

Hot tips

- Know how to use the camera. If you are a beginning photographer, use a "point-and-shoot" camera that is easy to use. If you are using a camera that you haven't used before, practise with several rolls of film. Ask for help if you need it.
- Be organized with your equipment. Make sure your flash works, bring extra batteries and film, and have somewhere safe to store your film.
- As you finish each roll of film, mark it with a number or subject name. That way, you won't reuse it and you'll know what's on it.
- During the photo shoot, take many shots of the same scene, but use different angles, lighting, and exposures.

How to Create a Photo Essay | 191

Read the title of this excerpt from a photo essay. What kinds of photographs do you think the essay will have?

Model

Aging Rockers — Do They Still Have What It Takes?

— title introduces the topic

Yesterday's stars are making music and earning a whole new generation of fans.

— deck catches the reader's attention

— close-up photograph gives the reader an immediate focus

There are definitely more gray hairs, but rock icon Neil Young hasn't lost any of his passion, talent, or flair for writing. His energy continues to affect the new fans who crowd his shows eager for the chance to keep on rocking in the free world.

— caption gives additional information

Think about It

Discuss with a friend why photographs and words are both important to a photo essay. What information does each give that the other cannot?

Use the Anthology

Read "New Views of the Cosmos" (pages 198-203) of the anthology. Write a paragraph to explain why a photo essay is an effective way to handle this topic.

Activities

1. Create a photo essay on a topic that interests you. Follow the steps on pages 189-190 of this handbook.

2. Choose a photo essay that a classmate has created. View it and then write a one-page essay about it. Discuss your essay with the author of the photo essay. Did you capture exactly what the author wanted to convey? If so, why? If not, what was missing?

Grammar

TABLE OF CONTENTS

Parts of Speech — 194
- Nouns — 195
- Pronouns — 197
- Verbs — 200
- Adjectives — 201
- Adverbs — 203
- Conjunctions and Prepositions — 205

Sentences — 208
- Sentence Structures — 208
- Common Sentence Errors — 210

Punctuation — 212
- Ending a Sentence — 212
- The Comma — 215
- Other Punctuation — 217

Connecting Words — 222

Direct and Indirect Speech — 225

Using Language — 228
- Synonyms — 228
- Antonyms — 230
- Homonyms — 231

Spelling Rules — 233

Parts of Speech

Before You Start

The different kinds of words that make up sentences, and so make up our language, are called parts of speech. The section that follows identifies many parts of speech, gives examples, and shows how to use parts of speech.

I love to be outside, so I hope that I can get a really interesting job working on a construction site this summer.

- love — verb
- so — conjunction
- that — pronoun
- can get — verb
- really — adverb
- interesting — adjective
- job — noun
- on — preposition
- summer — noun

Nouns

Before You Start

A noun is a word used to name a person, place, or thing. It can also name a feeling, such as fear. There are two kinds of nouns. Common nouns name a thing or group of things without being specific. Proper nouns are names for specific items. Here are some examples.

Common nouns

boy, woman, child, student, choir, home, forest, farm, joy, anger, food

Proper nouns

Nipissing University, Lincoln Alexander, Sioux Lookout, Pelee Island, Montreal Canadiens

MAKING NOUNS PLURAL

When naming more than one of the same item, use a plural.

To form the plural of most nouns:
- add 's' to the end of the noun

    dogs, legs, computers, pianos

To form the plural of a noun that ends in 's,' 'x,' 'z,' 'sh,' or 'ch':
- add 'es' to the end of the noun

    boxes, brushes, churches

To form the plural of a noun that ends in a consonant and then 'y':
- change the 'y' to 'i' and add 'es':

    parties, diaries

To form the plural of a noun that ends in a vowel and then 'y':
- just add 's'

    toys, keys

To form the plural of a noun that ends in 'f':
- change the 'f' to 'v' and add 'es'

    shelves, thieves

- sometimes, the 'f' doesn't change

    roofs, chiefs

Special plurals

- add 'es' to the end of *tomato, potato, hero, echo*:
  tomatoes, potatoes, heroes, echoes
- nouns that keep the same word for singular and plural, e.g.:
  deer, salmon
- nouns with unique plurals, e.g.:
  women, teeth, children

POSSESSIVE NOUNS

Nouns can show possession or ownership. Nouns that do this are called possessive nouns.

To form a possessive for a singular noun:
- add 's

  Massimo's car, the school's dress code

To form a possessive for a plural noun that ends in 's':
- add only an apostrophe

  dogs' bones, boys' shouts

To form a possessive for a plural noun that doesn't end in 's':
- add 's

  women's rights, choir's rehearsal

Act on It

Choose a selection from your anthology. Choose two paragraphs and identify all the nouns in the paragraph. Identify the kind of noun used and write the plural form of each word selected.

Apply It

Write several paragraphs on a topic of your choice. Include a variety of nouns that form their plurals in different ways. As a reference, use your rules for making nouns plural.

Keep at It

Complete Line Master 3 (available from your teacher) to support your understanding of how to pluralize nouns.

Pronouns

> **Before You Start**

A pronoun is a word that replaces a noun. There are two different kinds of pronouns. Personal pronouns refer to a specific person or thing. Indefinite pronouns do not refer to someone or something specific.

PERSONAL PRONOUNS

A personal pronoun refers to a specific person or thing.

There are three forms of personal pronouns: subject pronouns (who is doing the action), object pronouns (the person to whom the action is being done), and possessive pronouns (to show ownership).

Singular

Subject	Object	Possessive
I	me	my, mine
you	you	your, yours
he, she, it	him, her, it	his, her, hers, its

Plural

Subject	Object	Possessive
we	us	our, ours
you	you	your, yours
they	them	their, theirs

Using personal pronouns makes writing more interesting and prevents repetition. Read Model 1. What do you notice?

Model 1

Mia has always worked in the service industry. Because of this, Mia has developed excellent skills in dealing with the public. Mia is known for her ability to remain calm no matter how difficult the customer may be. Mia is well respected by her employer and by those with whom Mia works.

In Model 2, the noun, Mia, is replaced twice with "she." How does the change make the paragraph sound different?

Model 2

Mia has always worked in the service industry. Because of this, she has developed excellent skills in dealing with the public. Mia is known for her ability to remain calm no matter how difficult the customer may be. Mia is well respected by her employer and by those with whom she works.

INDEFINITE PRONOUNS

An indefinite pronoun doesn't refer to a specific person or thing.

These indefinite pronouns are singular. Use them with singular forms of verbs, and with the singular possessive pronouns 'his,' 'her,' and 'its.'

another	anything	everybody	neither
anybody	each	everyone	nobody
somebody	anyone	either	everything
no one	someone	any	

Each of the students has a textbook.
Nobody was in the gym when the lights went out.

These indefinite pronouns are plural. Use them with plural forms of verbs, and with the plural possessive pronouns 'their' and 'theirs.'

| both | few | many | several |

Few of the students cast their ballots.
Both of the children are eating their lunch.

These indefinite pronouns can be singular or plural. If they refer to one thing, they are singular. If they refer to more than one thing, they are plural.

| all | most | some | none |

Most of the cars on the lot are for sale.
Most of the audience thinks the movie is funny.
None of the crop is ready to harvest.
None of the votes were counted.

Act on It

Write a work-related incident report involving your description of the inappropriate behaviour of at least three people. Where suitable, use pronouns in place of nouns. Be sure that your pronoun references are clear.

Apply It

List the qualities that best describe the kind of person you feel would make an ideal employee. Write a paragraph of two to five sentences using only pronouns to describe this person.

Switch paragraphs with a partner. Rewrite one another's work about a specific person. How many pronouns will you keep in the passage?

Keep at It

Write several paragraphs to compare the style of dress of two different celebrities or other well-known people. Make sure you use nouns and pronouns properly. In small groups, share your writing. Be sure to check one another's work for proper usage.

Verbs

Before You Start

Every sentence has a verb. There are two kinds of verbs. A verb can be an action word that tells that something is, did, or will happen. A verb can also be a word that describes a state of being. The following are some examples of verbs.

Action words

shouted (*She shouted to her brother in the other room.*)
join (*Cliff will join us for dessert.*)
works (*Janine works for her mother.*)

State-of-being words

is (*My sister is an engineer.*)
seems (*The dog seems happy to see me.*)

Act on It

Read "Talking Toys Speak Volumes about Gender Stereotypes" (*Moving On*, pages 225-227). Choose at least five verbs used in the selection. Change the tone of the selection by replacing the verbs with different ones. Use a thesaurus to assist you. Discuss with a partner the changes you made.

Apply It

An incident occurred at work involving a very capable worker and a customer and her two young children. Write your view of the incident, which you witnessed. Use verbs that clearly define the behaviours.

Keep at It

Use the incident report you wrote, or any other piece of writing of your choice. Rewrite the passage, replacing the verbs. How does your rewrite change the tone of your writing?

Adjectives

Before You Start

There are several kinds of words that modify, or change, other words. We call these modifiers. One kind of modifier is an adjective. Adjectives are most often used to describe nouns, and are used in three different ways. Adjectives can show:

- which one

   this, that *(this student, that song)*

- what kind

   green, shiny *(green leaves, shiny surface)*

- how many or how much

   four, some *(four players, some animals)*

Most adjectives come before the word they are changing. A predicate adjective comes after a state-of-being verb, and modifies the subject of a sentence.

popular *(Soccer is popular all over the world.)*

Just as there are proper nouns, there are also proper adjectives.

Indian, English *(Indian food, English toffee)*

The adjectives 'a,' 'an,' and 'the' are called articles.

The job is perfect for me.

Act on It

Read "The Survival of the Fittest" (*Moving On*, pages 98-102). Identify at least 10 adjectives and the nouns they describe. Discuss with a partner the variety of adjectives used in the selection. Which adjectives indicate kind, colour, number, and size? Has the author included any proper adjectives?

Apply It

Write a description of a secret object using as many adjectives as possible to assist the reader in identifying what you are describing. Ensure that you use adjectives that appeal to all the senses by including the object's shape, colour, texture, and size.

Share your passage with a partner. What adjectives can your partner suggest to help describe the object more clearly?

Keep at It

Write a paragraph to describe the ideal setting for a graduation dance. Identify and describe the location, the decorations, the food, the music, and any other details you wish.

Adverbs

> **Before You Start**

Like adjectives, adverbs are modifiers. They add to the meaning of a word. An adverb tells how, when, where, or to what degree. Adverbs often come after verbs, to give more specific information about the verb.

quickly *(The tickets sold quickly.)*
tomorrow *(Mei Lin gets here tomorrow.)*
miserably *(He failed miserably.)*

The word 'very' is an adverb added to a modifier to further enhance the meaning of a verb.

Amy sings beautifully.
Amy sings very beautifully.

Many adverbs are formed from adjectives by adding 'ly' to the end of the word.

Adjective	**Adverb**
soft	softly
loud	loudly

There are exceptions, of course. The following are all adverbs that don't use 'ly.'

too   so   quite   rather   somewhat

The usage of the words 'good' and 'well' is often confused. 'Good,' an adjective, is always used to modify a noun.

Maniago is a good guitarist.

'Good' never modifies a verb, and almost never comes at the end of a sentence.

He did good. — incorrect
He did well. — correct

'Well' is usually an adverb, but can be an adjective. It almost always comes after a verb, or at the end of a sentence.

Sacha handles himself well in a crowd.
Maniago plays the guitar well.

Act on It

Read "Summer Wages" (*Moving On*, pages 152-160). Identify 10 adverbs that were used in the passage. What verb is each modifying? Change the adverb into an adjective with a noun that it modifies.

Apply It

Write a set of instructions for an activity (how to make a grilled cheese sandwich, how to skateboard). Use adjectives and adverbs to explain clearly each step in the process.

  Share your instructions with a small group. Ask for suggestions from the group to improve your description of the steps.

Keep at It

With a partner, write a dialogue where one person asks another to spend a summer weekend helping to build a community playground. Use adverbs and verbs to define the attitude of each person. Ensure that you each do not use the word 'said.' (See the list of words to replace 'said' on page 226).

Conjunctions and Prepositions

> **Before You Start**

Conjunctions and prepositions are connective words: they connect words, phrases, and paragraphs. When you add conjunctions and prepositions to your writing, you make your writing clear, logical, and interesting to the reader.

COORDINATING CONJUNCTIONS

The most familiar conjunctions are coordinating conjunctions — 'and,' 'but,' 'or,' 'yet,' 'nor,' 'so.' They show how two sentences work together. Use these words to join sentences and to show how they are related.

I enjoyed the holiday, but it was very expensive.
She backed out at the last minute so I had to ask Sam to take her place.

PAIRS OF CONJUNCTIONS

Some conjunctions work in pairs.

either/or, neither/nor, both/and, not only/but also, whether/or

Not only did she win, but she also broke a national record.
Whether I get the job in Halifax or Boston, I'm ready to make a move.
Neither the pigs nor the chickens have been fed.

SUBORDINATE CONJUNCTIONS

Subordinate conjunctions connect two clauses together. They show that one clause is more important than the other. Here are some commonly used subordinate conjunctions:

after	before	in order that	that	whenever
although	but that	lest	though	where
whereas	if	how	why	while
whether	unless	though	because	as
when	once	since	even though	than

I came to work this morning although I was here until 11:00 last night.
He walks faster than I do.
The union achieved the settlement because they had a lot of support.

PREPOSITIONS

Prepositions are also connective words. Along with joining words or groups of words, they show relationships between things.

Some prepositions show:
- general relationships

   about, for, from, like, of, with

   We went to the show with our friends.

- location relationships

   against, in, near, on, through

   I drove through the intersection and turned left.

- time relationships

   before, during, since, until, at

   I have had this job since November.

Act on It

Choose a selection from *Moving On*. With a partner, identify how the author has used prepositions. List the prepositions and identify them as showing general, location, or time relationships.

Apply It

With a partner, examine a newspaper article and list the prepositions used in the article. Identify the kind of prepositions used.

Keep at It

Choose a topic of interest to you and write a short essay that includes the following parts of speech:
— four adjectives
— three adverbs
— two coordinating conjunctions
— two subordinate conjunctions
— three prepositions – one of each kind

Exchange your essay with a partner. Identify the above parts of speech in one another's writing.

SENTENCES
Sentence Structures

> **Before You Start**
>
> A sentence has two basic parts: the subject and the predicate. The subject is the person, place, or thing that the sentence is about. The predicate contains a verb, and says, tells, or asks something about the subject.
>
> To create interesting writing, you need to use different sentence structures. A paragraph made up of only simple sentences is choppy and doesn't read smoothly. A paragraph made up of many complex sentences can be hard to follow.

SIMPLE SENTENCES

A simple sentence has only two basic parts: subject and predicate.

subject — *The boat sank.* — predicate

Both parts of a sentence can be compound, or have more than one part.

This sentence has a compound subject:

compound subject — *Neighbours and friends came to my party.*

This sentence has a compound predicate:

Eddie sang and played guitar. — compound predicate

COMPOUND SENTENCES

A compound sentence links together two simple sentences with words such as 'and' or 'but,' usually preceded by a comma. A semicolon can also link two sentences.

I'll meet you for lunch, but I have to finish my work first.

I've saved my money; I'm ready to buy the stereo.

COMPLEX SENTENCES

Clauses are groups of words that have both a subject and a predicate. Clauses that can stand alone are called independent clauses, or sentences. Clauses that can't stand alone are called dependent clauses. They need to be linked to a sentence, because by themselves they don't provide all the information the reader needs.

If you group together a main clause and one or more subordinate clauses, you create a complex sentence.

The manager called Gia whenever he needed someone to work overtime.
Although I didn't get the job, I did have a good interview.
Mario brought me soup because he knew I was sick.

Act on It

Read "The Metamorphosis of Lesra Martin" (*Moving On*, pages 58-67). With a partner, identify one of each kind of sentence in the passage. Change each compound or complex sentence to a simple sentence. Read the changes out loud. How does the passage sound? Now read aloud each sentence as it was written originally. Which version do you prefer? Why?

Apply It

Choose a set of instructions you have written (see Adverbs: Apply It, page 204). Identify any sentences that sound short and choppy and change them to compound or complex sentences. Add a compound subject or compound predicate where possible. Share your rewrite with a partner. Read the passage aloud. Discuss any differences in how it sounds.

Keep at It

With three other students, write a four-paragraph essay on a topic of interest to the group. One person writes the first sentence, then each other person takes a turn writing a sentence until the essay is complete. Use both simple and complex sentences, and vary their use to make the essay interesting. As a group, edit the essay, thinking about what you can do to improve it, including adding adjectives and adverbs where appropriate.

Common Sentence Errors

Before You Start

The most common sentence errors are the sentence fragment and the comma splice. Once you can identify them, you can fix them in your own writing. As you edit or peer edit your work, look at each place you have included a comma. Then check to see if you have made a comma splice error.

A comma splice error occurs when two statements are joined together incorrectly by a comma and should instead be two separate sentences, or should be linked using 'and,' 'but,' 'because,' or 'when.'

I have to walk to town, my car is out of gas. — incorrect; comma splice error

I have to walk to town because my car is out of gas. — correct

I have to walk to town. My car is out of gas. — correct, but overly simple and not very interesting

A sentence fragment error is a subordinate clause with no main clause to support it. It represents an incomplete thought. If you read the fragment, it will sound incomplete.

Because there was a storm. — sentence fragment error

Because there was a storm, Shoshi stayed at home. — correct

The roads were flooded because there was a storm. — correct

Act on It

Choose several pieces of your own writing. Circle any commas used. With a partner, determine if the comma has been used correctly or if you have created a comma splice (see The Comma, pages 215-216).

Apply It

The following examples represent incomplete thoughts or sentence fragments. Put these fragments in complete sentences and use them in a three-paragraph essay on a topic of your choice:

Because I needed some help.
Since I arrived here.
When I realized my mistake.

Keep at It

Work with a partner. One partner writes a sentence fragment. The other partner corrects the fragment by completing it. Change roles until you have written 10 sentences together.

PUNCTUATION
Ending a Sentence

> **Before You Start**
>
> All punctuation marks are signposts in writing that help readers know how to read a passage. Punctuation tells a reader when to pause and for how long, when to stop, when to consider a question, and when to feel strongly.
>
> There are several punctuation marks that you can use to end a sentence. They include a period (.), a question mark (?), and an exclamation mark (!). Ending punctuation should only be used with a complete sentence (see Common Sentence Errors, pages 210-211).

THE PERIOD

A period ends a sentence that makes a statement. When you are stating a fact, writing an opinion, or making a statement that has no great emotion attached to it, use a period. Most sentences end with a period.

The flowers bloomed in the garden.
Registration begins this afternoon.
I'll be home for dinner.

When you are using quotation marks, the period goes inside the end quotation mark.

"I'll do whatever I can to help."

Periods are not used to end titles, even if the title is a sentence.

No Great Mischief
Fall on Your Knees

THE QUESTION MARK

A question mark at the end of a sentence shows that the writer is asking for information.

Who can help Ling with her problem?
Why must we take this route?

When you are using quotation marks, the question mark goes inside the end quotation mark if the question is part of the quotation.

"Are you coming with us?"

Do use a question mark in a title if the title is a question.

Who's Afraid of Virginia Woolf?

THE EXCLAMATION POINT

An exclamation point is used to show strong feelings or emotions. Do not overuse exclamation points in your writing, or your reader won't know which information is really meant to show strong emotion.

"Stay away from me!" she shouted angrily.
The water was rushing right towards them!

When you are using quotation marks, the exclamation point goes inside the end quotation mark if the exclamation is part of the quotation.

"Stop that man!" the group shouted.

Act on It

From *Moving On*, choose a selection that includes direct speech. Change the tone of the speech by changing the words and punctuation used (for example, change questions to exclamations). How do these changes alter the meaning of the speech?

Apply It

Write questions to ask a partner about his or her favourite book or television program. Record the answers.

Then turn the questions and answers into dialogue. Rewrite your questions and your partner's answers, using verbs and adverbs that describe the way you and your partner spoke.

Check your punctuation to ensure that it describes how questions and answers were posed.

Keep at It

In your school yearbook, find a section about sports at your school. Read a text about any team or club, and then rewrite it as an interview with a player or coach from that team or club.

Share your rewrite with a partner. Ask your partner to change the verbs and adverbs where needed to indicate clearly the attitude of the speaker.

The Comma

Before You Start

The punctuation mark that people use most often in their writing is a comma (,). When it is used the right way, the comma helps readers understand what they are reading. A comma creates a short pause before a word or group of words. Commas can introduce information, separate ideas, or group ideas and information.

A comma can:
- introduce

    Danny, the handyman, can fix anything.

- introduce a question that a writer has

    Should I read this magazine now, or save it for the weekend?

- introduce the exact words that someone is saying

    Ravi asked, "Is this the tool you needed?"

- separate the name of a person to whom you are speaking

    Anita, can you tell me when you'll be finished?

- separate independent parts of a sentence that are joined by 'and,' 'but,' 'yet,' 'neither,' 'nor,' or 'or'

    It was raining hard, but the air was still warm.

- separate a group of descriptive words

    The red Mustang was old, rusty, unpredictable, and on its last legs.

- separate dates and places

    My new job starts on Monday, November 4, 2003, in Abuja, Nigeria.

- help make the meaning of a sentence clear by marking added information

    The rice, which has a nutty flavour, is the perfect addition to any meal.

Act on It

Using the rules for the comma on the previous page, dictate sentences to a partner to practise correct comma use.

Apply It

Find an example of comma usage in your own writing. Explain whether the comma has been used correctly or incorrectly, and how you know.

Keep at It

Use Line Master 4 (available from your teacher) to continue practising comma use.

Other Punctuation

> **Before You Start**

When you read, you come across different punctuation marks. The following is an explanation of the use of some of them, including the colon, semicolon, parentheses, dash, hyphen, and the apostrophe.

THE COLON

The colon has several different uses.

Use a colon:
- to precede a list

  Please bring the following:

  a sleeping bag
  a raincoat
  hiking boots
  a hat

- before a quotation

  The poster read: "Join the Army and see the world."

- in a very formal letter (for example, to a judge or a political leader), after the greeting

  Your Honour:

- to introduce an explanation

  It was a work day like most others this winter: up early to start up the trucks, then a day of plowing and shovelling with no time for breaks.

THE SEMICOLON

Semicolons create long pauses in your writing.

Use a semicolon:
- between two sentences that present related ideas

  Mom told everyone to buckle up; she wanted to start the car right away.

- to separate items in a list that contains other punctuation

    Shairose had many job offers to choose from: The Burger Joint, which gave her 40 hours a week but low pay; the drycleaner, which offered higher wages but fewer hours; and the convenience store, which gave her a flexible schedule.

PARENTHESES

Parentheses are used to enclose material that is not of major importance to the rest of a sentence, but that offers extra information.

He was an intelligent detective (one would hardly have suspected it from his appearance), well known for both his ingenuity and his daring.

THE DASH

A dash helps draw attention to key ideas in a sentence.

Use a dash

- to separate an explanation from the rest of a sentence

    The Toronto Marathon — run every fall — attracts huge crowds of both participants and spectators.

- to separate a series of words from a summary that will follow

    Dogs, cats, unique pets, farm animals — all of these are welcome to participate in the Sutton Fair and Horse Show.

- to show a sudden change of tone

    Cyril was friendly — suspiciously friendly.

THE HYPHEN

The hyphen has a variety of uses and a variety of exceptions to the rules.

Use a hyphen:
- after the word 'self' and the prefix 'ex' at the beginning of a word

    self-defence   self-interest   self-reliant   ex-fighter   ex-boyfriend

- to help distinguish the meaning of a word that might be confused with another word

    re-cover, not recover
    (re-cover a chair with new fabric rather than recover something lost)
    re-creation, not recreation
    (to create again rather than to have leisure time)

- to avoid using two e's or (sometimes) two o's together in a word

    re-enter   *re-examine*   *co-operate*

Spelling with Hyphens

Do not hyphenate:
- the following well-used compound words

    myself, yourself, himself

- these compound words

altogether	*anyone*	*basketball*	*baseball*	*bathroom*
bookmark	*cannot*	*daylight*	*farmhouse*	*fireproof*
forehead	*foresee*	*framework*	*grapefruit*	*handbag*
handwriting	*homework*	*notebook*	*nowadays*	*oneself*
outdoors	*overcharge*	*pillowcase*	*secondhand*	*semicolon*
snowstorm	*today*	*tomorrow*	*tonight*	

- a pronoun or adverb ending with 'body,' 'thing,' or 'where'

    anybody, somewhere, something

- points of a compass

    northwest, southeast

- a two-part word that includes an 'ly' adverb and comes before a noun to describe it

    smartly dressed man

These are always separate words

all right	*good night*	*high school*	*post office*
ranch house	*school year*	*school bus*	*will power*

Always hyphenate:
- the following words

    self-respect   *good-bye*   *re-enter*   *pin-up*

- any two-part word that comes before a noun and is used to describe it

high-strung	*so-called*	*left-handed*	*first-class*
old-fashioned	*well-bred*		

Do not hyphenate an adjective formed by adding 'like' to a one-syllable noun; do hyphenate if the noun has more than one syllable.

childlike   *doglike*   *business-like*   *tiger-like*

If you are unsure whether to hyphenate a word, look it up in the dictionary. If it is hyphenated, it should appear that way in the dictionary. If it is all one word, it should appear so in the dictionary. If it does not appear in the dictionary, write it as two separate words.

THE APOSTROPHE

An apostrophe is used to show possession, or is used in contractions to show that letters are being left out.

Possession

Use an apostrophe before the letter 's' to show possession for singular nouns or for plural nouns that don't end in 's.'

Mohammed's watch
the cup's handle
children's lessons
men's clothing department

Use an apostrophe to show possession for nouns that already end in 's.'

ladies' gloves
Oasis' size

Use an apostrophe before the letter 's' to show possession for indefinite pronouns.

anyone's guess
nobody's responsibility

Contractions

Use an apostrophe to show that a letter has been removed to create a contraction.

cannot — can't   *do not — don't*   *they are — they're*

Act on It

Review the rules of hyphen use. With a partner, test one another's spelling by dictating and writing a selection of hyphenated and non-hyphenated words.

Apply It

Look in a favourite magazine for examples of apostrophe use in the text or advertisements. List several uses, and describe the reason for each use. Have you found any errors in apostrophe use? Explain what makes them incorrect.

Keep at It

Write a four-paragraph opinion paper on a topic of your choice. Include the following:

- a semicolon
- a dash
- two hyphenated and two non-hyphenated words
- two words using an apostrophe
- three contractions

Circle the constructions used in your writing. Have a partner read your writing to ensure that you have used the above punctuation marks appropriately.

Connecting Words

Before You Start

One way to make your writing more interesting is to use a variety of sentences, including compound and complex sentences. Connecting words can help create these kinds of sentences. Connecting words link the ideas in various parts of a piece of writing by showing how those ideas relate.

Use connecting words within sentences.

Lots of great bands are playing at the festival, for example, Kittie, Peaches, and Dog Star.

Use connecting words between paragraphs.

… a need to begin to look at major changes.

On the other hand, we have far too many people requesting special consideration for this project.

Here are some connecting words and the relationships they show. You will notice that some of the connecting words are adverbs.

Use a connecting word:

- to list, add, introduce, or conclude

  to begin with, for a start, in the first place, first, second, third, and, also, for one thing, in addition, finally, lastly, in conclusion

  Also, I must thank all of those coaches who helped me prepare for the competition.

- to reinforce

  clearly, furthermore, moreover, besides, above all

  Clearly, we have to do something to help the homeless.

- to elaborate

  for example, for instance, to illustrate, such as, namely, in other words, that is

  There are people here who are responsible for the decorations, namely, the students in the art class, who gave up their lunch period to complete this work.

- to show similarity

  similarly, likewise

  Keena is an accomplished pianist. Similarly, his father excels at playing the organ.

- to show contrast

  instead, on the contrary, however, in spite of, on the other hand, yet, but, conversely, in contrast

  One puppy is active and eats well. Conversely, the other puppy is passive and uninterested in food.

- to show cause and effect

  thus, therefore, consequently, for this reason, because, since, accordingly, as a result, in order that, hence, so

  A major thunderstorm is expected later today. For this reason, the outdoor concert has been cancelled.

- to concede

  although, though, still, nevertheless, anyway, however, even though, even if, to be sure, granted that, whereas

  Although my aunt is 75, she refuses to give up sky-diving.

- to locate

  above, below, close by, nearby, next to, inside, opposite, within, without, further along

  The photocopier is next to the printer in the room at the end of the hall.

Act on It

Write a paragraph several sentences long to compare and contrast the clothes you wear in the summer and the clothes you wear in the winter. Be sure to include the appropriate connecting words.

Apply It

You are approaching the end of your high school years and are now beginning to think about the world of work. With a partner, list the advantages of being in school and the advantages of working. Independently, write a four-paragraph essay comparing work and school. Be sure to include appropriate connecting words to link your comparisons. Have your partner read your essay and highlight the connecting words you have used. Ask for suggestions to improve your essay.

Keep at It

In groups, share the two essays you have just written (in Apply It). Listen carefully to one another's work. How do connecting words help get ideas across clearly? Offer suggestions for connecting words that might help each writer.

Direct and Indirect Speech

Before You Start

In your writing, you may want to tell, repeat, or describe the words of a character or person. To do this, you need to know how to write direct and indirect speech.

DIRECT SPEECH

Direct speech refers to the exact words that a speaker says. Place the speaker's words within quotation marks.

The ambulance driver shouted, "I need help, now!"

When you are writing direct speech, begin a new paragraph for each new speaker. This helps the reader to know that the speakers are changing.

"The car is a complete write-off," stated Mr. Oxanich quietly.

"Dad, I'm sorry," replied Damon.

"I know you are, Damon. I'm just glad you're not hurt."

"Thanks for understanding, Dad," sighed Damon. "I'll work to pay you back."

If a quotation is divided by a reference to the speaker, use two sets of quotation marks, one set on either side of the reference to the speaker.

Here, the quotation is divided into two separate sentences.

"I'm so sorry," he answered. "I didn't hear what you said."

Here, the quotation continues the original sentence, so there is no capital on 'if.'

"It's hard to tell," she continued, "if I'm doing the right thing."

INDIRECT SPEECH

Indirect speech refers to reporting the words that someone said. The words may or may not be exact.

The ambulance driver said that he needed help right away.

Quotation marks are not needed for indirect speech.

CREATING VIVID DIALOGUE

When you write direct speech or dialogue, you need to show what is said and how it is said. Punctuation and effective word choices can help you write dialogue that comes alive on the page.

Use punctuation to show how words are spoken.

"Help!" yelled Parker.
"Help?" asked Parker. "Is help what you need?"

Instead of using the word 'said,' use active verbs and adverbs to further describe how a character feels while he or she is speaking.

"Help!" yelled Parker frantically.

Here is a list of words to replace 'said.'

commented	quipped	squeaked	argued	told
retorted	reminded	pursued	denied	exclaimed
supported	questioned	directed	demanded	asked
yelled	blurted	ordered	snorted	provided
cried	stammered	proclaimed	replied	shouted
uttered	roared	summoned	solicited	requested
interrupted	spoke	denounced	added	begged

Here is a list of adverbs that help add feeling to a verb.

smugly	politely	determinedly	quietly	worriedly
tersely	sheepishly	forcefully	meekly	boastfully
wryly	suspiciously	arrogantly	rudely	clearly
passionately	cruelly	happily	boisterously	forgivingly

Act on It

Read the selection "Making It Work Chat Room" (*Moving On*, pages 115-117). Chat room conversations are examples of direct speech. Discuss how chat room dialogue is different from dialogue you read in literature.

List the differences you have found and share them with group members.

Apply It

Create a 10-line dialogue between an employer and an employee who is late for work. Consider the personality and character of each person before you begin.

Use the list of affective adjectives on Line Master 5 (available from your teacher) to help you describe each person and how he or she might speak.

Keep at It

Read "The Interview" (*Moving On*, page 165). Use information from this poem to write a 10-line dialogue giving advice to a friend who found herself or himself in this situation.

USING LANGUAGE
Synonyms

Before You Start

One of the best ways to improve your writing is to vary the words you choose. If you want to find different words that mean the same thing, called synonyms, you can use a thesaurus. A thesaurus is a book containing lists of synonyms. It gives you a supply of words to use in your writing. You may find a thesaurus helpful if the word you have chosen doesn't quite say what you want it to say.

To use a thesaurus, look up the word that you want to replace. Then read the list of other words that have the same meaning. Sometimes the meaning is exactly the same; at other times, the words have a different feel or strength.

This paragraph shows the repeated use of the word 'dislike.'

I dislike the way you treat me. I dislike the attitude you have toward your work. Furthermore, I dislike the rude way in which you speak to customers.

In this paragraph, synonyms are used to replace the word 'dislike.'

I dislike the way you treat me. I disapprove of the attitude you have toward your work. I object to the rude way in which you speak to customers.

Act on It

Read "A Day No Pigs Would Die" (*Moving On*, pages 16-21). Look for descriptive words — adjectives that describe nouns, and adverbs that describe verbs. Replace each descriptive word with a synonym (see Line Master 5, available from your teacher).

Apply It

Write a four-paragraph descriptive essay that outlines the qualities you look for in a good friend. Write your essay using the language you would typically use. Then use the list of affective adjectives (Line Master 5, available from your teacher) to revise your work. Have a partner read your first draft and your revision, and offer any additional suggestions.

Keep at It

Write a three-paragraph evaluation of yourself as an employee or, if you do not have work, as a student. Use the list of affective adjectives (Line Master 5, available from your teacher) to assist you.

Antonyms

Before You Start

Antonyms are pairs of words that are opposite in meaning. When you are looking for the antonym of a word, be sure that it is the true opposite of the word.

Here are some antonyms.

good/bad	up/down	love/hate
success/failure	question/answer	competent/incompetent
superior/inferior	agree/disagree	employee/employer
true/false	dead/alive	whole/broken

You can make the exact opposite of a word by adding a prefix that means 'not,' such as 'un,' 'in,' 'im,' or 'dis.'

clear/unclear	professional/unprofessional	complete/incomplete
perfect/imperfect	service/disservice	

Act on It

Read the selection "All I Really Need to Know I Learned in Kindergarten" (*Moving On,* pages 112-114). Use antonyms to change the meaning of five sentences and give them the opposite meaning.

Apply it

Write a four-paragraph essay that describes the qualities you avoid in a friend. (This will be an essay that describes the opposite of what you wrote if you completed the essay for Synonyms: Apply It, page 228).

Keep at It

List 10 qualities that you think an employer looks for in an employee. With a partner, list the opposite of each word to create a list of the least desirable qualities in an employee.

Homonyms

> Before You Start

The most difficult thing about the English language is understanding that two or more words may sound the same but be spelled differently and have completely different meanings. These words are called homonyms. Here is one common example of homonyms at work.

***They're** cleaning the duckweed from the lake with **their** new machine, which is being docked over **there** by the red buoy.*

Why do all three words sound the same but have different spellings and meanings?

- **They're** is the contraction of the two words 'they' and 'are.'
- **There** is a directional word indicating a specific place.
- **Their** is a plural possessive pronoun used to show ownership.

Here is a list of some commonly used homonyms.

air – heir	him – hymn	principal – principle
aye – eye	its – it's	rain – reign
brake – break	flocks – phlox	their – there – they're
dear – deer	for – fore – four	time – thyme
dew – do	mail – male	to – too – two
cellar – seller	missed – mist	wait – weight
cite – sight – site	one – won	way – weigh
fair – fare	pail – pale	weak – week
grate – great	peace – piece	you'll – yule
hair – hare	plain – plane	
heal – heel	pray – prey	

Act on It

In your anthology selections, find several examples of words from the list of homonyms. In groups, test one another by reading the sentences and having group members write the correct spelling of the words based on the meaning.

Apply It

From the list of homonyms, identify the five pairs of words that are most challenging for you to remember. Write a sentence that uses each word correctly.

Keep at It

In pairs, test one another's spelling of the words in the list of homonyms. One person should dictate a sentence to demonstrate meaning, and the other person should correctly spell the homonym.

Spelling Rules

Before You Start

English is a language with nearly as many exceptions to its spelling rules as there are spelling rules. Here you'll find a few rules that, along with the other information in this grammar clinic, will help you with your spelling when you write.

DOUBLING A FINAL CONSONANT

Double the final consonant when you add a vowel suffix ('er,' 'est') to a word that ends in a single vowel followed by a single consonant (for example, 'big'), and that is one syllable or has the accent on the last syllable (for example, 'occur'). Here are some examples.

stop	+	ed	=	stopped
stop	+	ing	=	stopping
big	+	er	=	bigger
big	+	est	=	biggest
wit	+	y	=	witty
begin	+	er	=	beginner
begin	+	ing	=	beginning
occur	+	ed	=	occurred
occur	+	ing	=	occurring

DROPPING THE FINAL E

When adding a suffix, drop the final 'e' on words that end with a silent 'e.' Here are some examples.

dare	+	ing	=	daring
arrange	+	ing	=	arranging
admire	+	ation	=	admiration
fame	+	ous	=	famous
guide	+	ance	=	guidance

WORDS WITH 'EI' AND 'IE'

This poem might help you remember where to place 'i' and 'e' in a word.

'I' before 'e' except after 'c'
Or when sounded like 'a'
As in neighbour and weigh.

- so, 'i' before 'e':

    achieve		besiege		cashier		chief		grief
    mischievous	piece		relieve

- except after 'c':

    ceiling		conceive	deceit		receipt

- sounded like '*a*':

    freight		neighbour	reign		vein		weight

Some exceptions to the rules in the poem are these words.

weird, height, leisure, foreign, counterfeit, forfeit, heifer, sleight, species

Also when 'c' is pronounced 'sh,' 'c' is followed by 'ie.'

ancient, conscience, efficient, proficient, sufficient

Act on It

Make a list of words where the final consonant is doubled before 'ing,' 'ed,' or 'er' are added.

Review and discuss the rule with a partner. Then get in a group and list all of the words you have collected. Share all lists with the class.

Apply It

Write a sentence that clearly indicates the meaning of at least five of the words on the class lists created in Act on It.

Keep at It

In groups, discuss any words that you find challenging to spell. Practise spelling the words out loud. Finally, choose two words each, and test one another on oral spelling by leaving out letters for others to fill in.

Index

A
abstracts, 115, 116
acceptance, letters of, 74
action plans, 81–84
action words, 200
active verbs, in dialogue, 226
active voice, 90, 96, 111
adjectives, 201–202
    ending in "like," 220
adverbs, 203–204, 226
    as connecting words, 222
    ending in "ly," 219
    hyphens with, 219
advertising, 171, 182 (*See also* radio commercials)
affective level, in media, 170
agreement, letters of, 74
allusions, 57, 163
annual reports, 32–33
anthologies, citing articles from, 105
antonyms, 230
apostrophes, 220–221
appendix, 115
applications, job
    letters, 129
    reading, 9
articles (parts of speech), 201
audience
    language levels for, 163
    of media, 174, 175
    for oral presentations, 149
    of poetry, 122
    of presentations, 144
    of radio commercials, 186–187
    reaction to media, 182–185
    tone and, 91
    word choice and, 90
authors
    information about, 46
    perspective of, 43–48

B
bar graphs, 26
bias, in media, 178–181
bibliographic information, 100
    (*See also* citing sources)
bibliographies, 102
    (*See also* works cited)
body copy, in radio commercials, 187
body language, 135, 139, 141, 148
body paragraphs, 95, 115
bold (font style), 22
borders around text, 22
business reports, 32–34

C
cause and effect, 96
    connecting words to show, 223
CD-ROMs, 104
charts, 26
chronological order, 97
"chunking" of information, 139
circle graphs, 25
citing sources, 100–102
classification, 97
clauses, 209
clichés, 97
colloquial language, 126, 163
colons, 217
colour, 22, 175
commas, 215–216
comma splices, 210 (*See also* run-on sentences)
common nouns, 195
communication in groups, 156–161
comparisons, 163
complex sentences, 209
compound sentences, 208
compound words, hyphens with, 219
computers, revising on, 73, 90, 91
concession, connecting words to show, 223
concluding paragraphs, 95
conclusion, to reports, 115, 116
conflict, 64
conjunctions, 205–206
connecting words, 222–224
consonants, doubling final, 233
consumer choices, 178
contact sheet, 190
context, meaning from, 131
contractions, 220
contrast, 223
coordinating conjunctions, 205
covering letters, 74
critical listening, 140

D
dashes, 218
dates, 220
declining letters, 74
dependent clauses, 209
describing words, 54
description, 54–56, 163
design, of group product, 159
design elements, 21–24
diagrams, 26, 139
dialogue, 226
dictionaries, 129, 130, 132, 220
    personal, 129
direct speech, 225
discussions, in groups, 157
display type, 22
drafting, 72
    within groups, 159
    letters, 75
    reports, 116
dramatic irony, 57

E
"e," final, 233
editing (*See also* revising)
    within groups, 159
editorials, 46
"ei"/"ie," words with, 234
ellipsis, 101
e-mail letters, 77
emoticons, 77
essays
    familiar, 97
    formal, 97
    reading, 46
    revising, 97
    short, 95–99
    typing, 97
"ex-," 218
exclamation points, 213
explanations (*See also* instructions)
    colons introducing, 217
    dashes in, 218
explicit information, 37
eye contact, 135, 139, 148, 151

F
facts, 140
familiar essays, 97
fiction, themes in, 62

films, citing, 105
filmstrips, citing, 105
first person, 46
fonts, 21
    size, 22
    style, 22
formal business reports, 33
formal essays, 96
formal language, 126–127
formal letters, 74, 75
    colons in, 217
formal tone, 126
formatting
    instructions, 112
    workplace reports, 116
forms, 9

G
gestures, 135, 148
"good" *vs.* "well," 203
grammar checks, 73
graphic organizers, 157
graphs, 25–26
groups
    communication in, 156–161
    discussions, 157
    drafting in, 159
    final products of, 158–159
    information assessment in, 158
    key ideas in, 158
    product design in, 159
    recording information, 157
    research in, 159
    roles in, 157
    setting priorities, 157

H
highlighting, 18
homonyms, 231–232
hyphens, 218–220
    in lists, 22
    spelling with, 219

I
idea banks, for poetry, 120
"ie"/"ei," words with, 234
illustrations, 25
imagery, 163
images, 163
imperative mood, 111
implicit information, 37
inclusive language, 91

indefinite pronouns, 198, 220
independent clauses, 209
indexes, 17–20
indirect speech, 226
inferences, 37
informal language, 126–127 (*See also* colloquial language; slang)
informal letters, 74, 75
information, 37
    assessing, 158, 170–173
    "chunking," 139
    recording, 157
    visualization of, 139
instructions (*See also* explanations)
    oral, 134–137
    writing, 111–114
Internet, 86 (*See also* Web sites)
interviews, citing of, 104
introduction
    to essays, 95
    to reports, 116
irony, 57, 163
italics, 22

J
job applications
    letters, 129
    reading, 9

K
key ideas, within groups, 158
key points
    in listening, 139
    of reports, 116
key words, 12

L
language (*See also* slang)
    anti-discriminatory, 91
    colloquial, 126, 163
    formal, 126–127
    inclusive, 91
    informal, 126–127
    levels of, 126–128, 163
    in oral presentations, 148
    used in media, 175
legend, 27
letters, 74–77
    acceptance, 74
    of agreement, 74
    covering, 74
    declining, 74

drafting, 75
e-mail, 77
formal, 74, 75
informal, 74, 75
job applications, 129
of recommendation, 74, 106
revising, 75
sending, 75
thank-you, 74, 75, 106
typing, 75
libraries, 86
line graphs, 26
linking words, 90
listening skills, 138–142
lists
    colons preceding, 217
    connecting words in, 222
    hyphens in, 22
    numbers in, 22
    semicolons in, 218
literal level, in media, 170
literary devices, 163

M
magazine articles, 104, 105
manuals, 112
mass media, 168
meaning, 37
    from context, 131
    levels of language and, 128
media, 168
    affective level, 170
    analysis, 171
    areas of, 168
    assessing information from, 170–173
    audience, 174, 175, 182–185
    bias in, 178–181
    colour used in, 175
    language used in, 175
    levels of images, 170
    literal level, 170
    messages, 169, 172, 174
    music used in, 175
media aids, 152
memos, 78
metaphors, 122, 163
modifiers, 201, 203
multi-volume works, 104
music, in media, 175

N

narrative poems, 64
news media, 178
newspaper articles, 104
news reports, 171
"not," prefixes meaning, 230
nouns, 195–96
    ending in "s," 220
numbers, in lists, 22

O

open mind, in listening, 141
opinion pieces, 46
opinions, 140
oral instructions, 134–137
oral presentations, 148–152
    audience, 149
    delivery, 151
    outlines, 150, 152
    planning content of, 149
    purpose, 149
    rehearsals, 150–151
    research in, 150
    statistics in, 150
    topics, 149, 152

P

pamphlets, 104
paragraphs
    body, 95
    concluding, 95
parallel structure, 111
paraphrasing, 100, 101
parentheses, 218
parenthetical references, 101, 103
parts of speech, 194
peers
    feedback from, 89
    language levels for, 163
periods, 212
personal dictionaries, 129
personal pronouns, 197
personification, 122, 163
perspective, author's, 43–48
perspective, reader's, 43-48
photo essays, 189–192
pie graphs, 25
plans
    action, 81–84
    research, 85–88
plays, citing, 101

plurals
    of indefinite pronouns, 198
    of nouns, 195–196
poetic devices, 122
poetry
    narrative, 64
    themes in, 62
    topics, 120
    writing, 120–124
points of compass, spelling 219
portfolios, 106–110
positives and negatives, 96
possession, 220
possessive nouns, 196
predicate, 208
predicate adjectives, 201
prefixes meaning "not," 230
prepositions, 206
presentations, 143–147
present tense, 97
pre-writing, 72
problem-solution, 96
pronouns, 197–99
    hyphens with, 219
proper adjectives, 201
proper nouns, 195
publishing, of written work, 73
punctuation
    in dialogue, 226
    ending, 212–214

Q

question marks, 212–213
questions
    answering, 9
    asking, 139
    in presentations, 144, 145
    rhetorical, 145, 163
quotation marks
    exclamation points with, 213
    with paraphrases, 100
    periods and, 212–213
    with quotations, 101
quotations, 100–101
    colons before, 217
    short vs. long, 101

R

radio commercials, 186–188
    (*See also* advertising)
radio programs, citing, 104

readers, 162
recommendation, letters of, 74, 106
reference books, 104
reference librarians, 86
rehearsals, of oral presentations, 150–151
repetition, in presentations, 145
reports
    abstracts, 116
    conclusions to, 116
    drafting, 116
    introductions, 116
    key points, 116
    purpose, 116
    researching, 116
    revising, 116
    topics, 116
    workplace, 115–119
research
    finding information, 12–13
    within groups, 159
    listing materials, 102
    in oral presentations, 150
    plans, 85–88
    for reports, 116
résumés, 129
revising, 72–73 (*See also* editing)
    action plans, 82
    on computers, 73, 90, 91
    drafts, 89–94
    essays, 97
    letters, 75
    poetry, 121
    reports, 116
rhetorical questions, 145, 163
run-on sentences, 90 (*See also* comma splices)

S

sarcasm, 57
second person, 116
"self," 218
semicolons, 217–218
sentence fragments, 90, 210
sentences
    common errors, 210–211
    complex, 209
    compound, 208
    punctuation ending, 212–214
    run-on, 90 (*See also* comma splices)

simple, 208
structures, 208–209
subject of, 208
transitional, 90
variety of, 144, 222
series of words, dashes with, 218
shading, 22
short essays, 95–99
signature, on letters, 75
similarities and differences, 97
similarity, words to show, 223
similes, 122, 163
simple sentences, 208
situational irony, 57
size, of font, 22
slang, 163
slides, citing, 105
social groups, 183
social positions, 183
sources, citing of, 100–102
speaking
　skills, 148–152
　style, 143–147
spell checks, 73
spelling rules, 233–235
square brackets, 101
state-of-being verbs, 201
state-of-being words, 200
statistics, in oral presentations, 150
stereotypes, 178
storyboards, 190
stream of consciousness, 122
style
　guides, 102
　personal, 162
　revising, 73, 90
subject (of sentence), 208
subjects. *See* topics
subordinate conjunctions, 205–206
suspense, 49–53
synonyms, 17, 130, 228–229

T
table of contents, 12–16
tables, 26
television (*See also* media)
　citing programs, 104
　critical viewers, 178
　stereotypes on, 178
tense, present, 97
text arrangements, 22
thank-you letters, 74, 75, 106
theme(s), 43, 62–67
thesauri, 129, 130, 132, 228
thesis statements, 96
"they," use of, 91
"they're/there/their," 231
third person, 116
titles, of works
　in citations, 101
　periods and, 212
　question marks and, 213
tone
　for audience, 91
　change of, 218
　formal, 126
　of voice, 141, 163
topics
　oral presentations, 149, 152
　photo essays, 189
　poetry, 120
　reports, 116
transitional sentences, 90
two-part words, 219
typing
　essays, 97
　letters, 75

U
URLs, 105

V
values, 43
verbal irony, 57
verbs, 200
　active, 226
"very", 203
visual aids, 148, 150, 152
visualization, of information, 139
visual organizers, 157
visuals, 25–27
vocabulary, expansion of, 129–133
voice
　active, 90, 96, 111
　consistent, 90
　personal, 162–166
　tone of, 163
volunteering, 159
vowel suffixes, 233

W
Web sites, 86
　citing, 105
"well" *vs.* "good," 203
white space, 22
　in letters, 75
word-processing programs, 159
words
　choice of, 90, 91, 97, 126, 144, 162, 163
　describing, 54
　linking, 90
　series of, 218
workplace reports, 115–119
works cited, 102, 103–105
work status, 182
writing
　instructions, 111–114
　own voice in, 162–166
　poetry, 120–124
　process, 70–73
　publishing of, 73
　purpose, 162
　readers of, 162, 163
　stages in process, 70–73
　style in, 162

Acknowledgements

Every effort has been made to find and to acknowledge correctly the sources of the material reproduced in this book. The publisher welcomes any information that will enable it to rectify, in subsequent editions, any errors or omissions.

"Amnesty International Annual Report 2000." Copyright Amnesty International.

"Whose Story to Tell?" by Josie C. Auger. Reprinted from *Dimensions II*. Copyright © 1996 Gage Educational Publishing Company, a division of Canada Publishing Corporation.

"Bottom Drawer" excerpt from the novel *Bottom Drawer* by David Boyd. Copyright © 1996 Rubicon Publishing Inc.

"Planet Flare." Reproduced by permission of *Flare* Magazine.

"Judgement Day" by Jack C. Haldeman II. Excerpted courtesy of Spectrum Literary Agency, agent for the Jack C. Haldeman Estate.

Excerpt from *The Perfect Storm* by Sebastian Junger. New York: Harper Torch (an imprint of Harper Collins), 1997.

"Road Kill" by Claire Kerr. Reprinted by permission of the author.

"Man, You're a Great Player" adapted and excerpted from *Laughing with Lautens* by Gary Lautens. Reprinted by permission of McGraw-Hill Ryerson.

"Being a Witness in a Criminal Trial." Ministry of the Attorney General/The Queen's Printer for Ontario, 2002. Reproduced with permission.

"Overview of Ontario's Employment Patterns" from Ontario Job Futures 2000, Human Resources Development Canada.

"Minding their own business" by Kristin Rushowy, *Toronto Star*. Reprinted with permission — The *Toronto Star* Syndicate.

"What I Have Lived For" by Bertrand Russell. Courtesy of the Bertrand Russell Peace Foundation Ltd.

"What TV Does to Kids" by Harry Waters. Copyright © 1977 Newsweek, Inc. All rights reserved. Reprinted by permission.

Excerpt from "Ryan White: My Own Story" from *Ryan White: My Own Story* by Ryan White and Ann Marie Cunningham. Copyright © 1991 by Jeanne White and Ann Marie Cunningham. Used by permission of Dial Books for Young Readers, an imprint of Penguin Putnam Books for Young Readers, a division of Penguin Putnam Inc. All rights reserved.

"The Boy in the Burning House" excerpts from *The Boy in the Burning House* by Tim Wynne-Jones. Published by Groundwood Books.

Photographs

page 172: Getty Images, page 176: Digital Vision/Getty Images, page 191: Corbis